MATT AND T[

ULTIMATE
FOOTBALL HEROES

RASHFORD
KANE

FROM THE PLAYGROUND
TO THE PITCH

DINO

First published in the UK in 2021 by Dino Books,
an imprint of Bonnier Books UK,
The Plaza, 535 King's Road, London SW10 0SZ
Owned by Bonnier Books,
Sveavägen 56, Stockholm, Sweden

🐦 @dinobooks
🐦 @footieheroesbks
www.heroesfootball.com
www.bonnierbooks.co.uk

Text © Matt Oldfield 2021

Design by www.envydesign.co.uk

Paperback ISBN: 9781789465112

British Library Cataloguing-in-Publication Data:
A catalogue record for this book is available from the British Library.

Printed and bound in Great Britain by Clays Ltd, Elcograf S.p.A.

1 3 5 7 9 10 8 6 4 2

For Dylan – a current and future superstar

Matt Oldfield is an accomplished writer and the editor-in-chief of football review site Of Pitch and Page. Tom Oldfield is a freelance sports writer and the author of biographies on Cristiano Ronaldo, Arsène Wenger and Rafael Nadal.

Cover illustration by Dan Leydon
To learn more about Dan visit danleydon.com
To purchase his artwork visit etsy.com/shop/footynews

RASHFORD

TABLE OF CONTENTS

CHAPTER 1

UNITED'S PENALTY KING IN PARIS

6 March 2019, Parc des Princes, Paris

'A dreadful night for Manchester United' – that's what the newspapers said after PSG's simple first leg win at Old Trafford. 'They'll need a miraculous comeback now to keep their Champions League campaign alive.'

Not only were United 2–0 down as they travelled to Paris, but they were also missing three of their most important attackers. Anthony Martial and Jesse Lingard had both picked up injuries, while Paul Pogba had been given a red card.

What a disaster! That only left the manager, Ole

Gunnar Solskjær, with two fit and available forwards: Romelu Lukaku and United's local boy wonder, Marcus Rashford.

If anyone could save the day with a moment or two of magic, it was Marcus. He had done it many times before for United in the Europa League, starting at the age of only eighteen, so why couldn't he now do the same in the Champions League?

Marcus was ready to step up and shine. Under United's new manager, he had found his scoring form again, with seven goals already. In the Premier League, the FA Cup – now the Champions League would be next.

'Let's do this!' he told Romelu as they took up their positions on the pitch.

Although Marcus sounded as confident as ever, he knew that it wouldn't be easy. Even without Neymar Jr, the PSG team was still packed full of world-class talent: Gianluigi Buffon, Thiago Silva, Dani Alves, Marco Verratti, ex-United man Ángel Di María and, of course, Kylian Mbappé.

Back in 2017, Mbappé had beaten Marcus to win

the Golden Boy award for the best young player in Europe. Since then, he had also won two French league titles and the World Cup with France, as well as scoring his team's second goal at Old Trafford. Now, it was time for Marcus – and United – to bounce back.

As soon as the match kicked off, Marcus was racing around causing problems for the PSG defence. When Thilo Kehrer saw United's speedy Number 10 sprinting towards him, he panicked. His pass fell between Buffon and Thiago Silva, perfect for Romelu to intercept. *GOAL – 1–0!*

'Come on!' United's star strikeforce celebrated together.

Minutes later, Marcus used his pace and power to beat Kehrer to the ball and then tried to cross it to Romelu.

'Unlucky!' Solskjær clapped and cheered on the sidelines. 'Keep going!'

Again and again, Marcus was making Kehrer look like a fool, but unless it led to a goal, it wouldn't really matter. And when PSG equalised, that meant

United now needed to score three to win...

Marcus wasn't giving up, though. As he dribbled into the penalty area, he could hear Romelu calling for it in the middle. Cross or shoot? Cross or shoot? In the end, he couldn't make up his mind and got it all wrong. His mixture of cross and shoot curled well wide of the far post.

'Hey, I was here!' Romelu cried out near the penalty spot. He wasn't happy with his strike partner.

So the next time Marcus got the ball, he made up his mind straight away. Even though he was a long way from goal, he was going to shoot. BANG! He put so much whip and dip and swerve on the ball that it squirmed out of Buffon's gloves. And Romelu reacted first to pounce on the rebound. *GOAL – 2–1!*

'Nice one, Rash!' he high-fived Marcus as they ran back for the restart.

One more – that was all United needed now to pull off a miraculous Champions League comeback. Twice Marcus thought that he was through on goal, but both times the linesman's flag went up at the last second. *Offside!*

'Arghh!' he kicked the air in frustration. Time was running out.

And with ten minutes to go, it looked like Mbappé was about to end United's hopes. As he controlled the ball on the edge of the box, he only had David de Gea to beat, but somehow, he stumbled and fell.

Phew! Marcus breathed a big sigh of relief and then refocused his mind. The comeback was still on for United, if only they could create one last chance...

As Diogo Dalot ran forward from right-back, Marcus and Romelu were both in the box, hoping for a dangerous cross. Instead, the Portuguese defender went for goal. His shot deflected off a PSG player and flew high and wide. 'At least we've got a corner,' Marcus thought to himself, but Diogo thought differently.

'Penalty!' he screamed, pointing at his arm. 'Handball!'

Really? After a long and agonising wait while the referee checked VAR, at last it was given – a last-minute penalty for United!

Wow, it was a harsh call, but Marcus wasn't

complaining. Now it was his responsibility to step up and score to send United into the Champions League quarter-finals. As the PSG players protested, he tried his best to stay calm and focused. Put the ball in the net – that was all he had to do.

Marcus had been in high pressure positions like this before, most recently at the 2018 World Cup with England. He had scored in the shoot-out against Colombia; and now he had to do it again.

When the referee blew his whistle, Marcus started his well-practised penalty routine:

Four little shuffles to the left,
then short steps forward to try to fool the keeper,
and then *BANG!*

Buffon did dive the right way, but he had no chance of stopping it. Marcus had struck his penalty with way too much power; it was simply unstoppable.

Goooooooooooooooooooooaaaaaaaaaaaaaaaaalllllllllllll llllllllllllll!!!!!!!!!!!!!!!!!!!!!

'What a penalty!' Diogo shouted as he chased

Marcus over to the fans by the corner flag. Their comeback was complete.

And what a night. Marcus Rashford: Manchester United Champions League Hero was just the latest step in his amazing football journey. A journey that had started eighteen years earlier in his family's front garden.

CHAPTER 2

FRONT-GARDEN
FOOTBALL

From the very first time he saw it on TV, Marcus was mesmerised by football. As a baby in his mother's arms, he stared at the figures on the screen, wearing their red shirts and white shorts, running around a big green space, and kicking a small white round object. What was this weird and wonderful thing?

'Look Mum, he loves Manchester United already!' Marcus' big brother Dwaine cried out cheerfully.

Melanie smiled and held her youngest son up high like a trophy. 'That's my boy!' she said, looking lovingly at his happy little face.

The Rashfords lived in Wythenshawe, which was proud Manchester United territory, especially in the late 1990s. While their local rivals, Manchester City, were battling down in the second division, United were lifting the Premier League title for the fifth time, plus the FA Cup and the UEFA Champions League.

'I can't believe we won The Treble,' Dwaine marvelled, almost as if he had been one of the players out there on the pitch. 'What a club. What a season!'

United were the greatest team in England, and also the greatest team in the whole wide world. Well, according to Dwaine and Dane, anyway, and Marcus always believed his brothers.

They were his heroes, and as soon as he could walk, Marcus followed them around as much as he could. But there was one place where his mum wouldn't let him go – outside.

'See ya later, lil' man!' His brothers waved, closing the front door behind them.

Where were they going, and why couldn't he go with them? Marcus had spotted the football in Dwaine's hands. It looked like it came from that weird and wonderful game they had watched together on TV.

'Hey, wait for me – I want to play too!' Marcus decided, and he waddled over to the front door to follow them. But as hard as he tried, it wouldn't open.

'Woah, where do you think you're going?' Melanie appeared, scooping him up into her arms. 'Are you trying to escape again, Mister? Look, we can watch your brothers from the window...'

Dwaine and Dane hadn't gone far; they were just having a kickaround with their friends in the small front garden. While they showed off all their tricks and flicks, Marcus stared and stared, as if the living room window was another TV screen.

Front-garden football looked like so much fun! He couldn't wait for the day when he would be allowed to join in. But when would that be?

'Please!' he begged his brothers after his third birthday. They had been teaching him to kick and control the ball in the kitchen while their mum was out, but now he was ready to show off his skills *outside*.

But Dwaine and Dane both shook their heads.

'Sorry Marcus, not yet – you're still too young to play
with us big boys. Maybe next time, yeah?'

However, when the next time arrived, their
answer was still no. And the next time, and the next
time… It was so unfair – he was nearly four years
old now! So why couldn't he just join in for a little
bit of front-garden football? Marcus was willing to do
anything, even go in goal if he had to.

'Fine, you can play,' Dwaine gave in eventually,
'but no crying to Mum if you get hurt, okay?'

'Okay!'

And so, at last, Marcus's front garden football
career began.

At first, it was all a bit overwhelming for him. His
brothers and their friends towered over him and
charged around him like wild horses on that small
square of grass. It was as if Marcus wasn't even
there. Or as if he were an obstacle that was in the
way.

'Watch out!' the big boys warned, nearly knocking
him to the floor.

Marcus moved out of their path, but he didn't

walk away. This was front-garden football; he just needed a moment to get used to it.

'Over here – pass!' he desperately wanted to shout, but he was too shy to say it out loud. Plus, Marcus knew that if he did anything annoying, his brothers would send him back inside straight away. He really didn't want that.

'But at this rate, they're never going to give me a turn!' Marcus moaned to himself. He didn't give up, though. He soon swapped his gloomy frown for a fired-up glare. 'If I want that ball, then I'm going to have to win it for myself!'

Marcus would just have to be brave amongst the big boys. With a bold dart, he snatched the ball from under Dwaine's foot.

'Hey!' he complained. 'What are you playing at, bro?'

'It's my turn,' Marcus replied determinedly.

Right, now what? He had the ball, but if he didn't do something quickly, one of the big boys would steal it back. Marcus tried to remember some of the skills that he had watched them do through the window. This was his chance to show that he could do them too.

Flick! with his right foot,

Flick! with his left foot,

Flick! with his right knee,

Flick! with his left knee,

Flick pass! with his right heel, back to his brother.

'Not bad,' even Dwaine had to admit.

After that, the big boys changed their minds about Marcus. It turned out that he wasn't just an annoying little boy who was getting in the way; he was a talented young footballer, just like the rest of them.

'Here you go, Marcus – let's see what you've got!'

Soon, he was allowed to go with his brothers to the local Mersey Bank Playing Fields, although 'only to watch'. But while Dwaine and Dane were playing big eleven-a-side matches with their mates, Marcus practised his ball skills on his own on the sidelines, preparing for the day when he would be old enough to join a football team too.

CHAPTER 3

FLETCHER MOSS RANGERS

The Rashford family didn't have a lot of money, but they managed to find enough for young Marcus to go to football training. After all, it was his favourite thing in the whole wide world, and he was clearly very talented too.

'Good luck, son!' Melanie said, giving her youngest son a kiss. She had to go to work, so Dwaine would be taking Marcus along instead.

'Thanks, Mum!' he replied, buzzing with excitement.

Now that he was five, Marcus was old enough to join a local football club called Fletcher Moss Rangers. But first, he had to prove that he was good enough to play for one of Manchester's top youth teams. Wes Brown, the United defender, had started at Fletcher Moss, and now the club had a strong reputation for developing top young players.

'Top young players like me!' Marcus thought to himself on the way to the Mersey Bank Playing Fields.

He couldn't wait to get started. As his boots sank into the bobbly grass, it felt like he was taking the first step on a grand football journey. First, Fletcher Moss Rangers, then Manchester United and England, just like Wes Brown.

'Welcome, Marcus,' the coach, Mark Gaynord said, shaking his hand. 'I hope you're ready to have some fun today!'

Marcus nodded shyly, as a smile spread across his face.

'Great, then let's get started!'

Dwaine had played enough front-garden football with his brother to know that he was a promising young player, but he was curious to see how Marcus would compare against other kids his own age. It didn't take Dwaine long to see that his brother stood out high above the rest.

And the Fletcher Moss coaches saw it too. From the moment that Marcus first touched the ball, Gaynord could see that he had a natural gift for the game. It was as if he came alive with a football at his feet, his whole body suddenly working in smooth, skilful motion.

The head up, turning, looking out for defenders to beat and teammates to pass to.

The arms out, offering balance through all the twists and turns of the dribble.

The legs pumping, driving him goalwards at top speed.

The feet dancing, moving the ball with such grace and ease until at last, BANG!

Gooooooooooooooooooooaaaaaaaaaaaaaaaaalllllllllllllllllllllllllll!!!!!!!!!!!!!!!!!!!!!

Gaynord had coached many talented kids before, but no-one quite like Marcus. 'That boy is a superstar in the making,' the Fletcher Moss coach told himself, and he didn't doubt that for a second. The kid's ability was astonishing. Marcus had already mastered so many tricks and flicks at the age of five!

'How did he learn to dribble like that?' Gaynord asked Dwaine in awe.

'He probably saw me doing it in the park!' his brother said with a cheeky smile and then shrugged. 'Or maybe it was on FIFA, actually...'

Marcus just seemed to soak up football skills like a sponge, whether he was watching his heroes on TV, playing video games, or playing for Fletcher Moss Rangers in real life.

'That's it, yes – brilliant!'

As Marcus's coach, Gaynord soon gave up on teaching him the basics; he was already too good for that. Instead, he focused on finding ways to stop his young superstar in the making from getting bored because even in their twenty-minute matches, Marcus was scoring goal after goal after goal. Often, it looked more like a one-boy skill show than an actual football match.

'Okay, that's enough,' Gaynord would call out when the scoreline was starting to get embarrassing. 'Give some of the others a chance!'

At that stage, Marcus would drop deeper and

switch to setting up his teammates with assist after assist after assist. The Fletcher Moss coach felt sorry for the other teams they faced; they simply didn't stand a chance.

So, how could Gaynord help Marcus to become even better? By setting him new skills challenges to complete, the coach decided.

'So, have you been practising that Maradona spin I showed you?' he asked before kick-off.

Marcus had been working on it all week at the Mersey Bank Playing Fields and then back home in the front garden too. But he didn't all say that to his coach; instead, he just nodded calmly and confidently. Gaynord would just have to wait and see...

As soon as he got the ball, Marcus burst forward on the attack. He was over the halfway line and hurtling towards the penalty area when, at last, a defender came across to close him down...

Right, this was it! Usually, Marcus would dribble around his opponents, or just kick it past the defender and use his speed to reach it first. But not this time; no, he had a new trick to try out. Just

when it looked like he was going to crash straight
into the defender, Marcus dragged the ball back
with his right foot, spun his whole body around, and
dragged the ball forward with his left foot. *Olé!*

'Maradona Spin!' Gaynord thought to himself,
clapping even louder than usual.

Marcus was away, past the first tackle, but there
was another one on the way. No problem! He had
something extra up his sleeve to add to his coach's
challenge. As the second defender slid in, Marcus
dragged the ball back behind him and went the
other way.

'Cruyff Turn!' Gaynord gasped. It was
extraordinary. How had he learnt that trick too?!

The coach looked across at Marcus's mum, who
had managed to get the day off work to watch her
son play. 'I've never seen a kid that young play like
this before,' he admitted with an amazed look still
on his face.

Melanie just laughed. 'Oh come on, Mark – you
must see little superstars all the time!'

But the Fletcher Moss coach wasn't joking around,

or being dramatic; he was deadly serious. He had been involved in football all his life, so he knew what he was talking about when he said, 'No, honestly, your lad is going to play for Manchester United and England one day.'

CHAPTER 4

A HAT-TRICK FROM A NEW HERO

Marcus had to touch the red plastic seat behind him, just to make sure that it wasn't a dream. Yes, he really was at Old Trafford, about to watch Manchester United play!

'So, what do you think?' Dwaine asked as he lifted his brother up onto the seat so that he could see the huge green space below.

But Marcus didn't reply; he was too busy staring down at the players on the pitch, and spotting all of his heroes:

There was Ryan Giggs – Number 11,

Fletcher Moss's own Wes Brown – Number 24,

Ole Gunnar Solskjær – Number 20,

And their star striker, Ruud van Nistelrooy –
Number 10!

Hopefully, one day, he would be down there
himself, warming up for United.

Even if Marcus had heard Dwaine's question, he
wouldn't have been able to answer it. With so much
to see and soak up, he was lost for words!

And even if he had replied, his big brother probably
wouldn't have heard him anyway. The atmosphere in
the stadium was electric, with the 60,000 United fans
forming a noisy wall of red. Everyone was looking
forward to an exciting European night. Manchester
United were taking on Spanish giants Real Madrid in
the Champions League quarter-finals.

After losing the away leg 3–1, United had lots of
work to do at Old Trafford. But the belief was still
there, buzzing in the Manchester air.

Come On You Reds!

UNI-TED! UNI-TED!

As Marcus looked around and listened, he couldn't
stop smiling. Watching his favourite team live was
even better than he had imagined!

Although it was a great night for Marcus, it turned out to be a bad one for Manchester United. Their defence was destroyed by the best striker in the whole wide world – Ronaldo. Well, that was what Dwaine said, anyway, and after that night, Marcus agreed with his brother.

First, the Brazilian raced away from Rio Ferdinand and fired a swerving, dipping shot past Fabien Barthez. *1–0 to Real Madrid!*

Then he burst between the United centre-backs to get on the end of Roberto Carlos's cross. *2–1 to Real Madrid!*

And finally, he unleashed a long-range shot that rocketed into the top corner. *3–2 to Real Madrid!*

David Beckham came on for United and scored two goals to make it 4–3, but really it was Ronaldo's night. He was the hat-trick hero, and the best player on the pitch. Even the United fans had clapped when he scored that third thunderstrike.

'Fair play,' Marcus heard the supporters around him say. 'He's a class act, that Ronaldo!'

Marcus and Dwaine were both disappointed

that their team had crashed out of the Champions League, but they returned home with lots of stories and memories, and a new hero to admire.

'Bro, come and check this out!' Dwaine called out from the family computer.

Together, they spent many happy hours watching highlights of Ronaldo on YouTube. It didn't matter if he was starring for Barcelona, Inter Milan, Real Madrid, or Brazil. They were hooked. There were so many videos, so many goals, and – best of all, in Marcus's opinion – so many skills!

The silky taps of the ball,

the sudden bursts of speed,

the body swerves,

and, of course, the stepovers!

To the right, to the left, to the right again, then BANG! – GOAL!

Marcus was more mesmerised than ever. What a player! Out on the pitch, Ronaldo always looked so free – free to try new tricks, free to express himself and free to entertain. He made football look like so much fun.

'Let's watch the Lazio video again!' Marcus suggested almost every single night.

That was one of his favourite clips, from the 1998 UEFA Cup Final, when Ronaldo was playing up front for Inter Milan. They won 3–0 and the Brazilian scored a great goal, where he dribbled around the keeper. But that wasn't the part that Marcus really wanted to watch. No, he was much more interested in seeing the skills show.

'This is it… this bit now!' He pointed at the screen, his excitement growing.

Despite having a Lazio defender tackling him from either side, Ronaldo somehow kept hold of the ball, thanks to some really fast and fancy footwork.

Tap, tap, drag-back, turn, then an Elástico to escape…

And with another calm flick of the foot, he passed the ball onto his teammate.

'Unbelievable!' Marcus marvelled. No matter how many times he watched the clip, it just got better and better. Even when they tried to foul him, the Lazio defenders still couldn't stop him.

But how did Ronaldo do it? There was only one way to find out – time to practise! Marcus grabbed his ball and rushed out into the front garden. From now on, he was going to play the game just like his new hero, however long it took him to learn all the skills.

Marcus dribbled down the left wing and into the penalty area...

Stepover to the left, stepover to the right,

Stepover to the left, shift to the right...

BANG! – GOAL!

Marcus was through, one on one with the keeper...

Body swerve to the left,

Body swerve to the right...

Then, with the keeper lying fooled on the floor, he simply had to tap the ball into the empty net. *GOAL!*

'Wow, so where did you learn those new dance moves then?' his Fletcher Moss coach asked when he first showed them off at training.

'From Ronaldo,' Marcus replied proudly. 'He's my new favourite player now!'

CHAPTER 5

BUSY BOY

Word soon spread about the Little Ronaldo starring
up front for Fletcher Moss Under-7s. It wasn't just
his bright yellow shirt that was catching everyone's
eye. When the team won a big tournament in
Manchester, there was a whole crowd of scouts there
to watch Marcus. They came from top clubs all over
the north of England:

Newcastle,

Crewe,

Everton,

Liverpool,

Manchester City...

And, best of all, Manchester United!

So, was Marcus going to become the latest
Fletcher Moss player to move to Old Trafford? The
club's scout was certainly very impressed. The boy
wonder ticked all the right boxes:

✓ Skill
✓ Speed
✓ Good attitude
✓ Good awareness
✓ Great movement

That last one was really important, but luckily,
Marcus was a natural mover, who had also spent
hours watching and then copying his hero, Ronaldo.
So, with or without the ball, he glided across the
grass gracefully, with pace and power. Full marks!

Marcus was delighted when his favourite team
invited him to come and train at their Moss Side
development centre. 'Yes please!' he replied eagerly.

Suddenly, Marcus was a very busy boy, with a full
football schedule:

Training at Liverpool,

Training at Manchester United,

Playing matches for Fletcher Moss Rangers,

Kicking a ball around in the playground at Button Lane Primary School,

Kicking a ball around with his mates at Mersey Bank Playing Fields,

Oh – and a little bit of eating and sleeping in between!

'You must be exhausted after playing all that football,' Gaynord suggested to Marcus at the start of the Fletcher Moss training session.

But it didn't look that way as their young star got the ball and dribbled towards goal at top speed, his body swerving and his feet dancing. It was like there was no end to his energy!

It looked like there was no end to his ability either. The coach could already see that Marcus's time at Liverpool and United was turning him into an even better player. Back at Fletcher Moss, everything was far too easy for him. The other players might as well have been cones for him to dribble through; they had no chance of stopping him. Gaynord knew that it wouldn't be long before the boy left for good.

But where would Marcus go? Such a talented youngster had so many options. With both big Manchester clubs chasing him, he decided to try training at City too.

That might sound like a strange decision for a mad United fan to make, but the Rashford family had just moved to a new house. Their new home was now five miles away from United's training ground, The Cliff, and his mum couldn't drive. City's Platt Lane Complex, on the other hand, was just around the corner.

Platt Lane was so much easier for Marcus to get to, and it helped that Manchester City were desperate to sign him. The club had climbed back up to the Premier League and their manager, Kevin Keegan, was really giving their young players a chance. Shaun Wright-Phillips, Joey Barton, Nedum Onuoha, Stephen Jordan – they had all come through the club's academy and now they were starring for the first team.

'That could be you one day!' the City youth coaches told Marcus.

Although that was an exciting idea, Marcus was still secretly hoping to play for Manchester United one day.

He couldn't sign with any club until his ninth birthday, but as that day grew closer, United upped their efforts. They weren't going to let their local rivals, City, swoop in and steal such a top young talent. No way! There had to be something that they could do to keep Marcus at their club. If he was finding it hard to get to The Cliff, then they would just have to find another way to get him there…

'Of course, no problem,' Dave Horrocks, the Fletcher Moss chairman, said straight away when United asked if he could bring Marcus and his mum along to the club's main training ground.

Horrocks was always happy to help his young players, plus it was an amazing opportunity to visit The Cliff, the place where the famous 'Class of 92' had started their incredible football careers – David Beckham, Ryan Giggs, Paul Scholes, Nicky Butt, and Gary and Phil Neville.

'Are you excited, lad?' Horrocks asked in the car on the way to The Cliff. 'Because I am!'

On the back seat, Marcus nodded and smiled with his usual calm confidence. Yes, it was going to be a test, but a football test, not a maths test! There was nothing for him to worry about. He was excited, and he was ready to make his Manchester United dream come true.

CHAPTER 6

MADE FOR MANCHESTER UNITED

As he walked out onto the training ground pitches, Marcus felt a buzz flow through his body like a bolt of electricity. Mr Horrocks was right; there was definitely something special about this place. This was it – his big moment, training at the home of the mighty Manchester United. He was following in the footsteps of legends like Becks, Giggsy and Scholesy. Unbelievable!

Marcus wasn't letting himself get carried away, though. He knew that he still had a very long way to go if he wanted to one day become a United hero. This was just the start, the first step up from Fletcher Moss.

But it was going to be a very big step all the same – ginormous, in fact. At The Cliff, Marcus would be competing against lots of other amazing young attackers – the best in the city, maybe even the whole country. What if the club's youth coaches didn't think he was good enough? What if they decided not to give him a chance? All he could do was work hard and play his most impressive football.

'You've got this, bro,' Dwaine and Dane had told him before he had left home that morning. They believed in him, which made Marcus believe in himself too.

'Welcome to Manchester United!' the coaches said, shaking his hand and smiling warmly. 'Right, let's get you playing some football…'

Judging by that first training session, Marcus wasn't going anywhere – he was made to play for Manchester United! Their top youth coach, René Meulensteen, really believed in developing each player's individual skills for as long as possible, from the Under-7s all the way up to the first team.

'That's it – one touch to control. Now dribble forward through the cones, moving the ball from foot to foot, keeping it close to your boot… Brilliant, Marcus – well done! Come on lads, the new boy's showing you how it's done!'

It was the perfect environment for Marcus to learn and improve. Because instead of being told to pass the ball every time he touched it, he was encouraged to take his time, be creative and think for himself. What was the best way to get that ball in the net and win the game? He was free to try new tricks, free to express himself and free to entertain, just like his hero, Ronaldo.

'You looked like you were having fun out there today,' Horrocks said on the drive back home.

This time, Marcus didn't just nod and smile. 'Yeah, it was sooooo good!' he replied, the words bursting out of his mouth with joy. 'At first, I thought it was going to be a bit boring, but Coach got us doing all these really fun skills drills, and then we played a match, 5 vs 5, and I scored six goals, and then…'

Melanie was delighted to see her son looking and sounding so happy. After a few weeks of training with both Manchester clubs, Marcus knew, without any doubt, which training programme he preferred.

'I'll become a better footballer at United,' he told Horrocks. 'That's where I want to be.'

His family agreed, and not just because they were United fans. They worried that some other clubs might try to take away Marcus's unique playing style – the body swerves, the bursts of speed, the skills, the stepovers. But United wouldn't. At The Cliff, the coaches would get the best out of his amazing ability and turn him into a top, top player. Yes, Marcus was made for Manchester United.

'Right, United it is then!' Whenever he could, Horrocks drove Marcus to his training sessions at The Cliff. But when he couldn't, the boy had to make the adventure across Manchester with one of his brothers, or even on his own when he was old enough. Struggling with the weight of his heavy kit bag, he took one bus into the city centre and then another out to Salford. After a tough training session and a long bus ride back home, he would crawl into bed, happy but exhausted.

Luckily, that didn't last for too long. By the time Marcus officially joined Manchester United, aged nine, Dwaine had passed his driving test and bought a car to take him to training. Phew!

'Cheers, bro!'

'No problem. You can pay me back for all the petrol when you're earning £50,000 a week!' Dwaine joked.

Now, Marcus was all set to become a superstar in red, bringing goals and glory to Old Trafford. On the very day that he signed for Manchester United, it just so happened that the first team were training there at The Cliff. What were the chances? It was meant to be!

Van Nistelrooy, Solskjær, Scholesy and Giggsy – they were all right there, just a few pitches away, showing Marcus exactly what he was aiming towards.

CHAPTER 7

ROONEY AND THE NEW RONALDO

By the time that Marcus turned ten, however, he had
two more Manchester United heroes: Wayne Rooney
and the new Ronaldo.

Cristiano was Portuguese rather than Brazilian,
and he was a winger rather than a striker, but just like
the old(er) Brazilian Ronaldo, he loved to entertain
and show off his silky skills. In fact, out on the pitch,
Cristiano probably did even more stepovers.

'Woah, look at his legs go!' Marcus marvelled as
he watched YouTube videos with his brothers. As he
attacked with the ball, Cristiano's feet were a blur of
movement, dancing from side to side. It was all too
much for the dizzy defenders. GOAL!

Marcus did his best to copy 'Wazza' and Cristiano. As he was a United fan, they would have been his heroes anyway, but it certainly helped that he got to see them up close at The Cliff, working hard and getting better and better. Sometimes, Marcus would sneak into the gym and sit and watch Cristiano practising a certain skill on repeat until he had perfected it – jumping up for headers, taking free kicks. Didn't he get bored of doing the same thing again and again and again? No, because he was so determined to be the best.

That inspired young Marcus to keep practising his own skills as often as possible, whether he was:

Training at the United academy,

Challenging himself against Dwaine and the other big boys,

Playing all day long with mates his own age at the Mersey Bank Playing Fields,

Or even doing keepy-uppies with a tennis ball on the way to school.

Football was Marcus's favourite thing in the world, and with every kick and touch, he was working towards his Manchester United dream.

Just like his new hero, Cristiano – who on first arriving in England in 2003, had played for himself with all those fancy flicks and tricks. But five years later, he was playing for the team instead. His mind was focused on glory, and growing numbers:

Goals per season – 9, 12, 23!

Assists per season – 10, 9, 21!

Trophies – one FA Cup, one League Cup, two Premier League titles...

...and one Champions League?

Manchester United were through to the semi-finals of the 2007–08 tournament, and Marcus, like most United fans, was dreaming of European glory. He had only been two years old when the team won it in 1999, so this one would be extra special for him.

Come On You Reds!

UNI-TED! UNI-TED!

Five years on from the Brazilian Ronaldo's hat-trick hero performance, Marcus was back at Old Trafford to watch another big Champions League night. This time, United were up against the other

Spanish giants, Barcelona, and it was 0–0 going into the second leg. So no away goals scored, but none conceded either.

Come On You Reds!

UNI-TED! UNI-TED!

As the game kicked off, the atmosphere in the stadium was like nothing that Marcus had ever experienced before. It was as if the noise and passion of the fans was a physical force, pushing the United players forward, up the pitch, towards that final…

In the fourteenth minute, the new Ronaldo, Cristiano, dribbled at the Barcelona defence, weaving one way and then the other.

'Go on, go on!' Marcus urged his favourite trickster.

Gianluca Zambrotta did stop Cristiano eventually, but his clearance fell straight to Scholesy, who took one touch and then fired a wonderstrike into the top corner. 1–0 to United!

As the ball hit the back of the net, Old Trafford roared and rocked like it might fall down.

'Come on!' screamed Scholesy, down on the pitch.

And 'Come on!' screamed Marcus, up in the stands.

What a start! The next seventy-six minutes, however, were some of the most nerve-wracking and nail-biting of Marcus's young football life.

Edwin van der Sar saved from Lionel Messi. Yessss!

Ji-sung Park's shot went just wide. Noooo!

Carlos Tevez got past the Barcelona defence, but not past Víctor Valdés in goal. Noooo!

Van der Sar held on to Thierry Henry's header. Yessss!

Marcus kept looking up at the scoreboard, urging the seconds to pass. Surely, it was time for the referee to blow his whistle? At last, Rio Ferdinand headed the ball away to Tevez, who booted it up field… FWEEEEET – it was over!

'Yes, yes, YES!' Marcus yelled, hugging his brothers and anyone else he could find. What a victory – their team was through to another Champions League final!

It was a night that Marcus would never, ever forget. Those exciting European wins were why he was a Manchester United fan, and why one day, he was going to become a Manchester United hero too. Because if it felt that good just being a supporter, how good would it feel to be a player out there at the heart of the action?

Unbelievable – that was the answer! Marcus didn't really need any extra motivation, but it didn't hurt.

Three weeks later, things got even better. In the final in Moscow, United beat Chelsea 6–5 on penalties. It was another nail-biter for Marcus and his family but at least the right team had won in the end.

'Campeones, Campeones, Olé! Olé! Olé!' Marcus celebrated at home with his family.

United were the Champions of Europe, as well as the Champions of England! Marcus felt so proud to be a part of the club, and hopefully, its bright future. He vowed that, after Rooney and Ronaldo, there would be Rashford.

CHAPTER 8

GROWING UP FAST

One day at school, Marcus was asked to write about his dreams for the future. 'Easy!' he thought, picking up his pen. This was his favourite kind of classwork.

'I have one aim in life and that is to be a professional footballer, and hopefully at Manchester United.'

That was it; he wanted to make his family proud and make Old Trafford roar and rock.

As Marcus looked down at the words he'd written on the page, his goal suddenly seemed so simple. But actually, it was anything but simple. He was just one of millions of football-mad kids all over the world with exactly the same aim.

Marcus, however, had two key strengths

that helped him to stand out from the crowd at
Manchester United:

1) talent

and

2) determination

As he progressed through the club's academy,
Marcus stayed humble and Marcus stayed hungry.
Whether it was free kicks or his left foot, there
was always something that he wanted to improve,
something that he wanted to work hard on.

'Come on, time to go home, lad,' the United youth
coaches would tell him. 'We can practise that again
next week.'

It was Marcus's attitude that impressed the club
the most. That was why they decided to make him
their youngest ever Schoolboy Scholar, at the age of
just eleven.

'Wow, thanks!' was Marcus's first reaction when
the coaches told him, but that was before he started
thinking. Wait a second – what did becoming a
'Schoolboy Scholar' actually mean?

Well, the good news was that Marcus would get to

play a lot more football, even during school-time.

'Great, I'm in!'

But the bad news was that, in order to become a Manchester United Schoolboy Scholar, he would have to move schools and, more significantly, move away from home.

'Why?' he asked in surprise. He was only eleven! 'We don't live that far away, and Dwaine can just drive me there every day!'

Marcus wasn't sure that he was ready to leave his friends and family behind. Who would he have a kickaround with now? Where would he live – with strangers? And would he have to cook his own meals?

'No, there's a nice lady called Maria,' his mum explained, 'who has looked after lots of young Manchester United stars. You would be living with her, but don't worry, we will still see you all the time!'

Okay – if that's what it would take to achieve his one aim in life, then Marcus would do it. He was determined.

'Are you sure this is what you want?' his mum asked, as they arrived at Maria's house for a visit.

It was a big decision and Melanie couldn't help worrying about her little boy. After all, he was incredibly young to be away from home. But if this was what Marcus really wanted, then she wouldn't stand in his way.

By the end of the visit, she did feel a bit better about things. Maria was kind and friendly, telling stories about other Manchester United stars as she gave them a tour of the house.

'Gerard Piqué – yes, he could cause a bit of trouble, but bless him, he's a good boy really. He's gone back to Barcelona now, I hear…'

And for Melanie, it was also nice to know that her son wouldn't be staying there alone. There was another academy star living there too, another tricky winger in fact, called Tom Lawrence. He was three years older than Marcus, but they seemed to get on well straight away.

'Stick with me, mate,' Tom told him with a smile, 'and you'll be playing with the big boys in no time!'

Marcus loved the sound of that. Growing up with two big brothers, he was used to challenging himself against older, stronger, better players. And at the United academy, there were lots of those, especially in the Under-18s team.

Paul Pogba was a tall, talented midfielder from France,

Ravel Morrison was one of the most skilful players that Marcus had ever seen,

and Jesse Lingard was a lively little midfielder with an eye for goal.

Despite the big age difference, Marcus became friends with them. He was mature beyond his years and he wasn't afraid to introduce himself.

'Hi, is it true you used to play for Fletcher Moss?' he asked confidently.

Jesse smiled. 'Yeah, but only for a bit.'

'Cool, me too!' Marcus replied proudly.

It wasn't long until Manchester United's big boys were inviting him to join them in 'The Cage'. That's what they called their exciting freestyle football matches at the club's training centre in Carrington.

Paul McGuinness, their youth coach, thought it was a great idea.

'Just go a bit easy on him, okay?' he warned the older players. 'Remember – he's only twelve!'

McGuinness had a different message for Marcus, though. 'Show them what you can do, kid!' he said with a cheeky wink.

Sometimes, 'The Cage' was 11 vs 11, or even 13 vs 13, with chaos everywhere, and no space to take your time and think. Everything had to be done at super-speed – the skills, the shots, and most of all, the decision-making. Otherwise…

'Too late!' McGuinness would shout from the sideline. 'You need to play that pass earlier there, kid!'

'Yes, Coach!' Marcus would shout back, chasing after the ball again.

He was learning so much, with every minute that he played on the pitch. United's youngest-ever Schoolboy Scholar was growing up fast.

Sometimes, 'The Cage' was 7 vs 7, or 8 vs 8, which Marcus found way more fun. In those games, he had the time and space to really express himself, especially alongside such talented teammates. They made everything look so easy.

'Yes!' Paul called out for the ball.

As he played the pass, Marcus was already on the run again, demanding the ball back: 'One-two!'

When it arrived, he skipped past one tackle with a Ronaldo drop of the shoulder, then played another one-two with Paul. From the edge of the 'D', Marcus fired a fierce, low shot into the bottom corner. *GOAL!*

'Yes, mate!' Paul cheered as they celebrated with their special handshake.

On the sidelines, McGuinness clapped and smiled. The future of Manchester United looked very bright indeed.

CHAPTER 9

SIZE, STRENGTH AND SPEED

While Marcus seemed to be on a fast track to the top, he knew that in football, everything can change in an instant. One day, you could be the next big thing and a few weeks later, you could be the next one out the door. Marcus had seen it before. Between the ages of twelve and fourteen, many of his friends had left the Manchester United academy, for all kinds of reasons:

Too small,

Too slow,

Bad attitude,

Just not quite talented enough.

'Good luck!' they told him, moving on with no hard feelings.

For Marcus, it was always sad to say goodbye to teammates that he had played with for years. And it was also worrying – what if he was the next one to go?

But still, Marcus was determined to stay and become a Manchester United hero, even if that dream was starting to look more and more difficult. No-one doubted that he had the skill to succeed, and the willpower too, but what about the size, the strength and the speed?

Speed? Yes, speed! Before, Marcus had been one of the fastest players in the United youth team, but when his legs began to grow, his body struggled to keep up. As it tried to adapt, there was pain and there were problems slowing him down. Suddenly, he couldn't glide gracefully past defenders anymore. But why not? What was going on? It was like he had lost his football superpower.

'My career is over!' Marcus moaned dramatically as he trudged off the pitch after another frustrating performance. He was finding it hard to get into the game, and when he did, none of his skills seemed to work as well as they used to.

There was no way that he was going to become a top winger at United if he didn't retain his blistering pace. Perhaps he would have to move to a different position on the pitch, a position where speed wasn't so important. Maybe he could become a central midfielder instead, using his creativity and football brain...

No, no, no – United's youth coaches weren't going to let that happen. They knew that Marcus was made to attack.

'Hey, don't worry about your pace at the moment, kid,' the Under-16s boss, Neil Ryan, said, trying to lift his spirits. He had coached so many boys with growing pains before and he knew that the bad times wouldn't last. 'You'll get your speed back soon, I promise, but first, we need to work on your strength.'

Marcus certainly had the mental strength, but not the physical strength yet. Without that, he would never get his burst of speed back and big defenders would keep knocking him off the ball too easily. So, it was time for him to build up his core strength in the gym.

Planks, stomach crunches, bridges, leg raises, sit-ups… It was long, hard, boring work, but luckily for Marcus, his teammate, Axel Tuanzebe, was there to turn everything into a competition.

'Right, first to fifty press-ups wins… GO!'

Axel was already a big, strong defender, but Marcus hated to lose at anything, even press-ups. So their rivalry pushed him to improve. Once he set himself a goal, he would keep working until he achieved it.

'Yes, I finally won!'

Throughout those difficult times, Marcus kept smiling and thinking positively about the future. There was no point moaning or giving up on his dream. He just had to get on with his gym work and pass this test. It was all part of the process, part of his journey to the Premier League.

When Marcus saw other academy stars making it into the Manchester United first team, it inspired him to keep going:

First, Federico Macheda,

Then Danny Welbeck,

Then Tom Cleverley,

And then in 2011, Marcus's mates from 'The Cage' – Paul, Ravel and Jesse.

If they could all do it, then so could he!

Marcus also found extra motivation at the 'Theatre of Dreams'. He was there watching in the Old Trafford crowd when Dimitar Berbatov scored a heroic hat-trick to beat Liverpool 3–2, and when Rooney scored a brilliant bicycle-kick to win the Manchester derby against City.

'That's going to be me one day!' Marcus kept telling himself. That's what he was working towards, and it would all be worth it. He could do this; things were going to get better. Size, strength and speed – he would need all three to become a superstar like his United heroes.

'That's it, kid,' Ryan encouraged him. 'Keep battling for that ball!'

Marcus was a young man on a mission. Day after day, he got a little bit bigger, a little bit stronger, and a little bit faster again.

Just after his fifteenth birthday, he got his first England call-up, to play for the Under-16s in the Victory Shield against Wales. Next to Dominic Solanke and Joe Gomez, Marcus looked so tiny, but he didn't let that stop him.

'Well done, kid!' Kenny Swain, the manager, congratulated him after a brave and battling performance. Even on a tough night, Marcus had still shown moments of magic, moving so beautifully with the ball. It was easy to see the boy's huge potential, but he still had some developing to do.

By the time he turned sixteen, Marcus had also experienced his first taste of training with the United first team. What an amazing experience it was, to be up close and personal with proper Premier League stars! He barely touched the ball all session, but that didn't matter. What mattered was that he was making progress.

He was far from being the finished footballer yet, but his youth coaches weren't worried about that. They now knew that he had the hunger and determination to overcome any setback. The rest could wait. The club was happy to be patient with Marcus as his body grew, because this was a boy who was destined for Manchester United greatness.

CHAPTER 10

FROM NUMBER 10 TO NUMBER 9

Yes, Marcus was destined for Manchester United greatness, but what position would he play? After starting out on the right wing, the academy had moved him all over the attack: left wing, striker, Number 10. So, where would he play his best football?

That was the hot topic amongst the club's youth coaches. They'd had a similar problem a few years earlier with another ex-Fletcher Moss forward: Danny Welbeck. Was he a winger or was he a striker? In the end, they left it too late to decide and they didn't want to make the same mistake with Marcus.

'The kid's got too much talent to just stay up front and shoot,' some argued. 'That's not his style. He wants to be on the ball all the time!'

That was true; Marcus was really enjoying life in the Number 10 playmaker role. Buzzing around behind a striker, he had a lot more space and time to use his number one weapon: skills!

But not all of his coaches saw it that way: 'No, he looks like a classic modern striker to me. He's fast, he's going to be at least six feet tall and he can dribble with the ball too. Surely, he's more Thierry Henry than David Silva, isn't he? There's only one thing missing at the moment – goals.'

Marcus did score goals for the United Under-16s, but to become a top Number 9, he would need to start scoring a lot more often. So it was time for some special striker lessons.

'Instead of dropping deep to collect the ball, we want you racing in behind the defence,' the Under-18s coach, Colin Little, taught him in training. 'It's all about getting yourself in the right position, and then timing your run to perfection. Let's give it a go.'

Marcus loved learning new things, especially when it came to football. So, he practised bursting into the box again and again, from every angle.

'Yes!' he called out, pointing forward to where he wanted the pass to go.

'That's better!' Little encouraged him. 'If you're sprinting onto a through-ball at top speed, no centre-back in the world is going to catch you.'

That was only the first part of the striking process, though. Once Marcus had the ball on the half-turn, he had to learn to be lethal. *TOUCH, BANG!.. GOAL!*

'Don't over-think it when you're in those positions,' Little told him. 'It's all about instinct and finding your rhythm. Just picture the goal, pick your spot and SHOOT!'

Marcus wasn't a natural finisher like van Nistelrooy, but he was always willing to work hard to improve. He read all the guides that his coaches gave him and then asked them lots of questions.

'So, let's say Dev is dribbling down the wing. Should I make a run to the near post, or between the centre-backs?'

'If Axel is looking to play a long ball out from the back, should I move out wide into the channels, or stay in the middle and try to win the flick-on for Callum?'

McGuinness and Little were delighted to see their young star taking striking so seriously.

Marcus also watched hours and hours of highlights from the best strikers in the business: Sergio Agüero at Manchester City, Luis Suárez at Liverpool, and of course, his old United hero, Cristiano Ronaldo at Real Madrid. Just like Marcus, Ronaldo had started out as a skilful playmaker, but he had turned himself into a super striker instead. He had just scored sixty goals in a single season!

Marcus could only dream of getting that many, but it was great to see Cristiano combining skills with goals. Maybe he would enjoy being a top striker, after all! Soon, it was time for him to put his lessons into practice on the pitch. Could Marcus shine as Manchester United's new Number 9?

At the start of the 2014–15 season, his youth coaches made a wise decision. They kept him in the Under-18s squad, rather than sending him up into the Reserves.

He was ready to play at a higher level, but there was no rush for him to compete against big, bruising defenders. Why not let him build up his confidence first, against smaller, less experienced centre-backs?

It took him a few games to get going, but eventually Marcus found his scoring form in the Under-18 Premier League. He finished the season with thirteen goals in twenty-five starts.

'He's really starting to look like a striker now!' McGuinness and Little agreed excitedly.

At the Mercedes-Benz Junior Cup in Berlin, Marcus scored two goals, plus a penalty in the final shoot-out, as Manchester United lifted the trophy.

'Hurraaaaaaaay!'

In the 2015 UEFA Youth League, the coach, Nicky Butt, made Marcus captain. In his first game against PSV Eindhoven, he scored a penalty and then burst into the box to convert Tyler Reid's cross. *One game, two goals!*

And what about the FA Youth Cup? The Class of '92 had won the competition, and so had Paul, Ravel and Jesse in 2011.

Marcus knew that it was the perfect place to make a name for himself. He scored a stunning free kick against Tottenham during his first tournament, and he was an even better striker second time around.

As Callum Whelan collected the ball just inside the QPR half, Marcus was already on the move, between the centre-backs.

'Yes!' he called out, pointing forward to where he wanted the pass to go.

Marcus was through, one on one with the keeper, but as he dropped his shoulder and dribbled around him, the keeper clipped his legs. Penalty!

Marcus picked himself up, and then rushed over to pick up the ball. That spot-kick was his. He was United's Number 9 now, and he was going to score. After a slow run-up, he blasted the ball into the back of the net.

Goooooooooooooooooooooaaaaaaaaaaaaaaaaalllllllllllll llllllllllllll!!!!!!!!!!!!!!!!!!!!!!

'Get in!' Marcus was really starting to love that scoring feeling. And with every strike, he was getting closer and closer to his target – the Manchester United first team.

CHAPTER 11

DREAM DEBUT I

'Today, we had Marcus Rashford on the bench,'
Manchester United manager Louis van Gaal told
the media after their Premier League match against
Watford in November 2015. 'He's a fantastic talent.'

Wow, what a wonderful thing to hear! Marcus
didn't make it onto the pitch that time, but still,
he got to sit with Sergio Romero, Marcos Rojo and
Andreas Pereira on the bench. And best of all, he
had his own squad number now – 39. It even had
a '9' in it!

That season, United were really struggling for fit
strikers. They still had Wayne Rooney, plus Anthony
Martial and youngsters James Wilson and Will

Keane, but they were often out ill or injured. So, who else could they call on?

'Me, me – pick me!' Marcus tried to show his manager whenever he got the chance to train with the first team.

After all, van Gaal was famous for giving young players a chance. He had handed Clarence Seedorf, Patrick Kluivert and Edgar Davids their debuts at Ajax, then Xavi, Andrés Iniesta, Carles Puyol and Víctor Valdés their debuts at Barcelona. The Dutchman clearly had a good eye for spotting future superstars, so who had impressed him at Manchester United so far?

The club's youngsters found out the answer in February 2016, when Wayne, James and Will all had to miss United's Europa League second leg against FC Midtjylland. Anthony would start up front, with Jesse and Memphis Depay on the wings, but they'd need some back-up on the bench. So van Gaal decided to include his favourite young striker in the squad.

'Mum, I'm in – I made it!' Marcus shouted proudly into his phone.

He couldn't believe it – what an incredible opportunity for an eighteen-year-old! United were 2–1 down after the first leg in Denmark, so there was a good chance that, in this second leg, Marcus might be needed to help attack later in the second half.

In fact, he was needed a whole lot sooner than that. As the squad warmed up at Old Trafford, one United player pulled up with an injury. It was Anthony. Uh oh, what were they going to do without their top goal scorer? Move Memphis up front and then Juan Mata to the left wing? No, van Gaal wanted to play with a proper striker.

'Rashford, get ready – you're starting!'

Starting? For the Manchester United first team? At Old Trafford? Oh boy, this was *BIG!* It was a good thing that Marcus didn't have much time to think about it. Kick-off was only minutes away.

'Just play your natural game tonight,' van Gaal instructed him. 'Express yourself – show the world what you can do.'

'Mate, you're gonna be great!' Jesse told him in the tunnel.

Marcus nodded. He was a little nervous, of course, but mostly excited. His childhood goal was about to come true. They didn't call it the 'Theatre of Dreams' for nothing! All those striking lessons with Little, all those goals for the Under-18s – they were preparing him for this massive moment. He just had to stay calm out there and make the most of any opportunities that came his way.

'Marcus who?' some of the United supporters asked each other when they saw the final team sheet. But they soon knew all about their new star striker.

In the fifteenth minute, Morgan Schneiderlin dribbled into the Midtjylland box.

'Yes!' Marcus yelled to his left, not afraid to call for the ball. He took one touch to control it, and then thought about the shot straight away. His strike was powerful and on target, but a defender blocked it.

'Good effort!' his United teammates encouraged him. 'Keep going, kid!'

With Old Trafford urging him on, Marcus never stopped moving. Sometimes, he appeared on the left, sometimes on the right, and sometimes in the middle. Midtjylland had no idea how to mark him! When his team had possession, Marcus ran into space to make himself available for the pass. And when they didn't, he chased after the defenders to win the ball back. He wanted it all the time.

From a throw-in, Marcus turned and attacked the penalty area at speed. With a left-foot stepover, he made space for the shot… *BANG!* The ball was travelling towards the bottom corner, but the keeper dived down to push it wide.

'Unlucky!' he heard Jesse clap and cheer.

Marcus was getting closer and closer to a debut goal. He could feel his confidence growing with every touch. He was playing with freedom, like he was just in the park with his mates. He even dared to do a cheeky backheel one-two with Juan. The United fans roared with delight. They loved him already! The tricks didn't always come off, but at least Marcus was brave enough to try.

It was 1–1 at half-time, meaning 3–2 to Midtjylland on aggregate. United needed goals in the second half, and soon.

A cross from the right flew over Memphis's head, but Juan just managed to keep it in. He cut the ball back to the edge of the six-yard box, which seemed to be empty... but wait! Marcus had the speed of thought and the speed of foot to get there in a flash. With a cool side-foot, he passed the ball into the net. 3–3!

Goooooooooooooooooooaaaaaaaaaaaaaaaalllllllllllll llllllllllllll!!!!!!!!!!!!!!!!!!!!!

Old Trafford was rocking, and it was all because of Marcus. What a feeling – words couldn't describe it! He raced over to the corner flag and into the arms of the celebrating fans. Only a few weeks earlier, he had been a Manchester United supporter, just like them. Now, he was also a Manchester United scorer.

'Great stuff, Rash,' the captain, Michael Carrick, congratulated him. 'Right lads, let's get another goal!'

And who was most likely to score it? Marcus, of course. Every time he touched the ball he looked so dangerous.

As Guillermo Varela looked up to cross it in from the right, he saw Marcus with his arm up, waiting in space near the penalty spot. United's Number

39 followed the flight of the ball carefully and then placed his shot past the keeper. 4–3!

Goooooooooooooooooooaaaaaaaaaaaaaaaallllllllllll llllllllllllll!!!!!!!!!!!!!!!!!!!!

Marcus ran over to celebrate with the same supporters again. What a night! Was this really happening? He had imagined his Manchester United debut many times before, but this was way beyond even his wildest dreams.

It was a very special, proud moment, not just for Marcus, but also for his friends, family and for all the coaches who had helped him along the way, from Fletcher Moss Rangers and then through the United youth teams – Gaynord, Horrocks, McGuinness, Ryan, Little. They had all believed in the little boy wonder, and just look at him now!

Although he couldn't quite complete his hat-trick, Marcus was undoubtedly the man of the match. A new United hero had been born – and all because of an injury in the warm-up.

CHAPTER 12

DREAM DEBUT II

The days of 'Marcus who?' were over. Suddenly, everyone was talking about the eighteen-year-old striker who had just bagged two goals on his Manchester United debut. He was now the club's youngest-ever scorer in Europe, beating the great George Best's record. And it wasn't just the goals; it was also the skill, the speed, the style, the energy. Marcus had already created a buzz of excitement.

So what next for United's new young star? With the pressure on, would he prove to be a one-game wonder like Macheda, or was he the real deal?

It didn't take long for the fans to find out. With United's injury crisis continuing, three days later,

Marcus found himself once again in the starting line-up. This time, he would be making his Premier League debut, against Arsenal. Wow, it was a good thing that he was such a cool, calm character.

'More of the same, yeah Rash?' Jesse joked in the dressing room before kick-off.

Marcus smiled back confidently, 'I'll see what I can do, mate!'

He tried to stay relaxed for as long as possible, but once he heard the passion of the fans and felt his feet touch that Old Trafford pitch, his mind was fully focused. Focused on winning, and hopefully, scoring some more goals.

Come On You Reds!

UNI-TED! UNI-TED!

Right from kick-off, United were the team on top, and once again, their new Number 39 was the player to watch. The Arsenal defence just could not cope with Marcus's speed and movement. When he got the ball and burst between two of them, all they could do was bring him down. *Free kick, just outside the box!*

'That's it, mate!' Memphis shouted. 'Keep running at them – they're scared of you!'

Marcus nodded – dribbling at defenders was what he loved best. But he wasn't all about skills anymore; he was also a goal scorer now. So if Arsenal switched off for even a second, he was ready to pounce like a proper Premier League striker...

In the twenty-ninth minute, Gabriel Paulista got to Guillermo's cross first, but the Arsenal defender couldn't clear it properly. In fact, he passed it straight to Marcus, who had stolen in at the back post. He didn't even take a touch to control it. In a flash, he curled a powerful shot past the keeper and into the top corner. 1–0!

Goooooooooooooooooooaaaaaaaaaaaaaaaalllllllllllll llllllllllllll!!!!!!!!!!!!!!!!!!!!

That amazing adrenaline rush again.

'Yes, you hero!' Juan screamed, throwing his arm around Marcus as they ran together towards the corner flag. He was certainly part of the team now.

'What a life-changing three days for Marcus Rashford!' the TV commentator cried out.

Two goals on his United debut, and now one on his Premier League debut too – Marcus was on fire! As he leapt into the air in front of the fans, he didn't think that life could get any better.

But there was more to come. Three minutes later, Jesse chipped a dangerous ball into the Arsenal box, aiming for United's new star striker. Marcus had positioned himself perfectly, just like Little had taught him: in between the centre-backs.

'Go on, kid!' the fans urged, growing more and more excited in their seats.

Marcus still had plenty of work to do, though.

He wasn't the tallest of strikers, but he timed his jump brilliantly, keeping his eyes on the ball floating towards him.

Jesse's cross didn't have that much power on it, but Marcus used his neck muscles to swing his head around and nod it down into the bottom corner. *2–0!*

Goooooooooooooooooooooaaaaaaaaaaaaaaaalllllllllllll llllllllllllll!!!!!!!!!!!!!!!!!!!!

'You couldn't make this up,' the commentator cried out again in utter disbelief. 'This is truly astonishing!'

'Thanks, mate!' Marcus yelled, racing over to give Jesse a big hug. After scoring all those goals together in 'The Cage' when they were younger, they knew each other well, but it was a dream come true to now be doing it at Old Trafford, and for the first team.

Two games, four goals – and still, United's new star striker wasn't finished. He kept running and fighting and calling for the ball. He wasn't playing for himself; he was playing for his team.

When Arsenal's attacker Mesut Özil whipped the ball into the box, it was Marcus who was back there to clear it away.

And when their keeper Petr Čech received a back pass, it was Marcus who rushed forward to close him down.

Later in the second half, when Marcus found three Arsenal defenders blocking his path in the penalty area, he didn't try to trick his way through. Instead, he took his time, looked up and spotted Ander Herrera running forward, calling for the pass. 3–1!

'Thanks, Rash!' Ander yelled as the United players all celebrated together.

After two goals and one assist in eighty magical minutes, Marcus's day was done. As he walked slowly off the field, every United supporter was up on their feet, applauding and chanting his name.

Rashford! Rashford! Rashford!

It was a very emotional moment for Marcus, but just like when he got the ball in front of goal, he looked so cool about it. Nothing fazed him at all. He just calmly climbed the steps to the subs bench, handing out high-fives on the way to his seat.

Pressure? What pressure? Marcus was loving life in the Manchester United first team. He had the self-belief, and also the talent to back it up.

'In my experience, youngsters often play well in their first match,' van Gaal said afterwards, 'but the second is different. Marcus did well in his second match, so he's a special talent, I think.'

It was clear to van Gaal that Marcus had already proved himself; surely now it was easy for everyone else to see that he was definitely the real deal.

CHAPTER 13

MANCHESTER DERBY MAGIC

After his two dream debuts, Marcus's next games for Manchester United were underwhelming. His next five games for the club passed without him scoring a single goal. Oh dear, was the kid going to be a two-game wonder, after all?

Of course not! Although he was disappointed, Marcus didn't let his head drop. He kept working hard in training and listening to the older teammates around him.

'Don't worry. At your age, you're going to have good days and bad days,' Wayne Rooney reassured him. 'I definitely did, anyway!'

Marcus was glad to hear that, especially from a

United legend and one of his childhood heroes. Wayne knew exactly what it felt like to be the 'next big thing' in English football – all of the hype and the pressure. He had only been sixteen when he scored that wondergoal for Everton against Arsenal.

'You've just got to ignore all the talk and stay focused on your football,' Wayne continued. 'That's my advice, not that you need it. You're gonna be great!'

When the day of the Manchester derby arrived, Wayne was still out injured. That meant another start for Marcus in attack, less than a month after his club debut. This time, he had to score. He couldn't go SIX games without a goal – he was meant to be United's new star striker!

As he prepared for the big game, Marcus watched the video of Wayne's brilliant, derby-winning bicycle-kick, from back in 2011. He had been there in the Old Trafford crowd to witness that amazing moment. Now, five years later, it was Marcus's turn to try and become a Manchester derby hero.

'Come on, I can do this!' he kept telling himself.

A lot had changed since 2011, however. City were now two-time Premier League Champions and their team was packed with talent. Sergio Agüero, David Silva, Jesús Navas, Raheem Sterling, Yaya Touré – they had an experienced attack worth millions and millions!

The United attack, on the other hand, was all about youth and potential. Jesse was twenty-three, Anthony was twenty and Marcus was eighteen. They hadn't even played fifty Premier League games between them! So, what could they achieve together, away at the Etihad Stadium?

For the first fifteen minutes, Marcus mostly watched from the halfway line as City attacked again and again. Navas fired his first shot wide and then his second straight at David de Gea.

'Focus!' The United keeper clapped and cheered as he organised his teammates to defend the corner-kick.

Marcus could already tell that he wasn't going to get many chances to score that afternoon. Oh well, that just meant that he would have to be a more clinical striker.

And a smarter striker too. He wasn't having much luck on the left against the pace and power of Eliaquim Mangala and Gaël Clichy, so Marcus switched to the other side.

At last, United brought the ball forward, out of their own half. As Morgan Schneiderlin passed it through to Juan, Marcus positioned himself between City's other two defenders: centre-back Martín Demichelis and right-back Bacary Sagna.

This was a key part of United's game plan. If Marcus could just get himself one-on-one with Demichelis, he knew that he could destroy the Argentinian with his speed and skill. The plan had nearly worked the first time, and now Marcus was ready to try again.

Anthony made the run down the wing, to drag Sagna out wide. This was it – United's best opportunity to score.

'Yes!' Marcus called out for the ball. He was feeling even more confident now. It was time to show off those fast feet with a moment of Manchester derby magic.

With his first touch, he controlled it,

With his second, he attacked,

And with his third, he slid the ball through Demichelis' legs.

NUTMEG! Marcus was through, one on one with Joe Hart.

'Go on, go on, go on!' the United fans urged, jumping to their feet.

The pressure was on, but Marcus didn't panic. He wasn't going to waste this huge chance. Everything seemed to slow down around him, but he was in the zone, in total control of the situation. He took his time, picked his spot and then slotted the ball past the City keeper. *1–0!*

Goooooooooooooooooooooaaaaaaaaaaaaaaaaallllllllllllll llllllllllllllll!!!!!!!!!!!!!!!!!!!!

What a cool, calm finish in his first-ever Manchester derby! It was his new favourite goal *EVER*.

'Yessssssssss!' Marcus was bursting with pride as he raced into Anthony's arms. He had done it – he had scored a goal against their greatest rivals, City! Soon, he had Jesse jumping on his back too.

'Mate, that was ice-cold!'

Marcus had scored on his United debut, then on his Premier League debut, and now on his Manchester derby debut. He was a big game player, that was for sure.

The next seventy-five minutes were long and nervy for United, but at least Marcus was out there playing on the pitch, rather than watching from the stands. Could he grab a second goal to make things more comfortable?

Before half-time, Marcus ran onto Morgan's flick and tried to dribble past Demichelis again. Just as he was about to skip past him, the defender cut across him and clipped his legs.

'Penalty!' Marcus cried out as he fell to the floor, and so did every other United player and supporter in the stadium.

The referee, however, shook his head. What?! As Marcus got back up, the City defenders surrounded him, accusing him of diving.

'No way!' he defended himself fiercely. Cheating wasn't his style. 'I'm not a diver!'

The City players were trying to make Marcus lose his temper, but he wasn't falling for that. By the time

the game restarted, he was calm and focused again.
No problem, he would find another way to win the
game for United.

He kept dribbling at Demichelis until eventually
City had to take him off early in the second half. It
was safer that way; Marcus was causing him too
many problems.

United's Number 39 was tireless and fearless; even
when Marcus got cramp, he carried on fighting for his
team. In the last seconds of the match, he dribbled
the ball forward from deep in his own half, all the
way up to the corner flag. Mangala did tackle him in
the end, but his run had relieved the pressure on the
United defence and wasted some valuable time.

'Great work, Rash!' Jesse called out when he
caught up with him at last.

At the final whistle, Marcus was exhausted, but
also emotional. What a day! He shook his head in
disbelief. Unbelievable! The last thing he needed was
Jesse jumping on his back again, screaming in his ear:

'Mate, we did it! We won The Derby –
Manchester is RED thanks to you!'

Others might have become arrogant at that moment, but not Marcus. He stayed humble and hungry. The next day, he was back at school as normal, studying for his BTEC, as if he hadn't done anything special at all.

CHAPTER 14

TROPHY TIME

Two goals on his United debut, two more on his Premier League debut and now the winner in the Manchester derby – could Marcus's breakthrough season get any better?

Yes, if he could win a team trophy! Wasn't that what every player wanted most of all? United were already out of the League Cup and the Europa League, plus they were down in sixth place in the Premier League. So the only competition left was the FA Cup, which they hadn't lifted for twelve years.

'Come on, let's make that trophy ours!' said the captain, Michael, urging on his teammates. As a club legend, he was used to winning lots of silverware.

United's chances of lifting the FA Cup were looking good until they drew 1–1 with West Ham at Old Trafford in the sixth round. Now, they would need to win the replay at the Boleyn Ground. That didn't sound too difficult, but other than that famous Manchester derby victory, United's away form was awful. Still, with Marcus, Anthony and Jesse all there in attack, anything could happen...

Early in the second half, Anthony burst forward with the ball and slipped it through to Marcus on the edge of the West Ham box. DANGER ALERT! He had one defender in front of him and three more chasing from behind, but Marcus had been practising his best Brazilian Ronaldo impression for years.

Tap, stepover to the left, shift to the right...
BANG! – TOP CORNER!

Goooooooooooooooooooaaaaaaaaaaaaaaaaalllllllllllll llllllllllll!!!!!!!!!!!!!!!!!!!

'Mate, what a strike!' Anthony congratulated Marcus with a high-five and a hug.

Together, they were forming a very promising strike partnership, with so much pace and skill.

It was Anthony who grabbed the winner against
Everton in the semis to take United through to the
FA Cup Final.

'Get in!' Marcus cheered loudly as the team
celebrated in front of the fans at Wembley.

A month later, United were back there at 'The
Home of Football' to take on Crystal Palace, and
hopefully, to end their season on a high.

For Marcus, it was his first taste of that special
Wembley Cup final atmosphere. Wow, what an
experience! As the two teams walked out onto the
field, they came face-to-face with the sights and
sounds of 88,000 supporters.

Come On You Reds!
We all Follow the Palace!
UNI-TED! UNI-TED!
EAG-LES! EAG-LES!

Marcus had already played in the Manchester
derby, in European nights at Old Trafford and also
away at Anfield, but this felt even bigger. That's
because there was a top trophy up for grabs.
Winning the FA Cup would be the perfect way to

end his exciting first season at United. 'Eighteen games, eight goals and one trophy' – yes, that sounded so much better.

So Marcus started the 2016 FA Cup Final like a hero in a hurry. After a clever one-two with Wayne, he dribbled all the way down the left wing and into the Palace penalty area. He almost escaped past Damien Delaney, but at the last second, the defender cleared the ball out for a corner.

'Come on!' the United fans roared, feeding off the energy of their young striker.

Soon, he was at it again, this time on the right wing. With a clever dummy, Marcus skipped straight past Delaney at the second attempt. As he carried the ball forward, he looked up and spotted Anthony running in at the back post. The cross was good, but the shot was bravely blocked.

'Unlucky!' Michael clapped and cheered from midfield. 'Keep going!'

Unfortunately, those were Manchester United's best moments in a poor first half. They were struggling to find a way past the strong Palace defence. It was going to take a moment of magic, and Marcus looked the most likely player to create it. He felt confident enough to try his full range of tricks, even in a big Wembley final.

Early in the second half, Marcus thought he'd finally managed it. With a classy flick, he slipped the ball through to Marouane Fellaini, who struck it fiercely first time towards the top corner... *BACK OFF THE RIGHT POST!*

'Ohhhhhhhh!' Marcus groaned along with 50,000 others.

Eight minutes later, Anthony's glancing header flew towards the bottom corner... *BACK OFF THE LEFT POST!*

So close again! And that was as close as United got to a goal while Marcus was still on the pitch. In the seventy-third minute, he jumped up for a header and landed awkwardly.

'Argghh!' he cried out, clutching his right knee down on the grass.

Marcus was desperate to carry on playing, but he couldn't. The pain was just too intense. With a sad shake of the head, he hobbled off the pitch and straight down the tunnel to the dressing room.

What a disappointment, especially when he was playing so well in a cup final at Wembley! Five minutes later, things got even worse, when Palace took the lead. Nooooooo!

'Come on, United!' Marcus muttered under his breath as he lay there on the treatment table.

Luckily, his teammates fought back straight away. Marouane chested down Wayne's cross and Juan volleyed it in: 1–1 – back in the game!

The excitement and drama carried on in extra-time. When Chris Smalling was sent off, it didn't look good for United. But five minutes later, their super sub, Jesse, volleyed home the winning goal.

'Get in!' Although it was hard not joining in with the team celebrations, Marcus was so happy for his best mate. After the final whistle, he limped over in his team tracksuit for their special FA Cup Final handshake.

'Yes, JLingz – I knew you'd score today! The tekkers on that strike, eh?'

Together, they climbed the Wembley steps to collect their winners' medals. Then, after a short wait, it was trophy time for United.

'Hurraaaaaaaay!' the whole team cheered as Wayne and Michael lifted the FA Cup high above their heads.

What a day, what a season! Marcus still had to pinch himself sometimes, just to check that he wasn't dreaming. His breakthrough year at United felt too good to be true.

And hopefully, as long as his injury wasn't too serious, his sensational season wasn't over yet. Because even though Marcus hadn't made his England debut yet, the manager, Roy Hodgson, had just named him in his squad for Euro 2016.

CHAPTER 15

EURO 2016

When he first heard the news, Marcus couldn't believe it. 'Me, going to Euro 2016 with England, at the age of eighteen?' he thought to himself. No way, someone must be playing a nasty joke on him. One of his mates? One of his brothers?

But no, it was true, it was really happening! After his amazing first half-season at United, Marcus was about to become an England international, and maybe play for his country at a top tournament. Unbelievable!

'It's mad – I haven't even played for the Under-21s yet!' he told his family, shaking his head with a mixture of disbelief and delight.

Ahead of Euro 2016, everyone knew England's

top three strikers: Wayne Rooney, Harry Kane and Jamie Vardy. However, in Hodgson's squad, there was space for four forwards, maybe even five. So, the national team manager had some difficult decisions to make. Should he go for an experienced goal scorer like Jermain Defoe or Daniel Sturridge, or an exciting young maverick like Marcus?

England had a history of taking their best young attackers to major tournaments. Wayne had gone to his first one at the age of eighteen, as had Michael Owen and Alex Oxlade-Chamberlain, while Theo Walcott had been picked in the 2006 World Cup squad at the age of seventeen.

So why shouldn't Marcus be next at Euro 2016? Some argued that it was too soon for him, but others could see that he was ready to shine.

'I think Marcus Rashford will go to the Euros,' said former England striker, Ian Wright. 'He has pace, he makes super runs and he finishes comfortably: He's got everything.'

In the end, Hodgson selected Marcus and Daniel in his first squad of twenty-six, but England would only be able to take twenty-three players to the tournament. Three would be left behind, but who would they be?

Not Marcus! No, he was determined to impress his national team manager, both on the training field and also in the pre-tournament friendlies.

He didn't play in the 2–1 win over Turkey, but with Daniel injured, Marcus made his England debut against Australia at the Stadium of Light in Sunderland. Right, he thought, time to shine!
In the second minute of the match, left-back Ryan Bertrand played the ball up to Marcus, who passed it over to Raheem Sterling on the wing.

'One-two!' Marcus called for it back, in space just inside the penalty area.

Raheem decided to go for the cross instead, but the ball bounced off the Australian defender and looped up in the air...

Marcus was onto it in a flash. As it dropped, he calmly volleyed it past the keeper. *1–0!*
Goooooooooooooaaaaaaaaaaaallllllllllllllll!!!!!!!!!!!!!
It was another debut goal for Marcus, and this time for his country. It was unreal – he hadn't even been

on the field for three minutes! With his arms out wide, he raced over to the corner flag to celebrate.

'Mate, you've got that magic touch!' Raheem shouted, with a big smile on his face.

Marcus grinned back at his new teammate. Hopefully, Hodgson would see that too.

His dream England debut lasted sixty-three minutes, and before he was subbed off, he also helped set up the second goal for Wayne.

Jordan Henderson's pass was coming straight towards Marcus, but at the last second, he heard a shout from Raheem, who was racing up behind him. So with a drop of the shoulder, he dummied the ball and let it run through to Raheem, who crossed it to Wayne. 2–0!

It was high-fives all round for England's new attack. Surely, Marcus had to go to the Euros now?

'I'd take him,' his United captain, Michael, told the media. 'He brings something different.'

Marcus didn't play at all in their last friendly against Portugal, but when Hodgson selected his final England squad, his name was there on the list.

'Mum, I'm in!' he shouted down the phone. 'I made it – I'm going to France!'

Things were moving so fast for Marcus that he found it hard to take it all in. He had dreamed of playing at the 2018 World Cup and Euro 2020, but never Euro 2016.

'This is crazy!' he thought to himself, as he set off on his latest football adventure.

Marcus knew that he wouldn't be starting for England at the Euros, but hopefully he would at least get the chance to be a super sub once or twice.

He stayed on the bench for the first game against Russia, but in the second against Wales, England were drawing 1–1 with twenty minutes to go.

'Marcus, you're coming on!' one of the coaches called out.

Yes! He raced onto the pitch, ready to become England's super sub. In the end, however, it was Daniel who did that job instead, playing a one-two with Dele Alli and then poking the ball into the bottom corner. *2–1!*

As Marcus celebrated the goal with the others,

he couldn't help wishing that he had been the hero.
Still, the main thing was that England were winning.
He had to be a team player and wait his turn.

'Nice one, Studge!'

Having taken his chance against Wales, Daniel got
to start the last group game, and the Round of 16
game against Iceland. Marcus, meanwhile, watched
most of the match from the bench.

'Come on, England!'

After a confident start, the team totally collapsed.
From 1–0 up, they went 2–1 down, and it was like the
players had forgotten how to pass the ball. What was
going on? If they didn't start playing properly soon,
England were heading for a humiliating early exit.

For Marcus, it was so hard to just sit there and
do nothing. He wanted to help turn things around,
but instead he fidgeted on the bench while Hodgson
brought on Jack Wilshere and then Jamie Vardy...

There were only five minutes left, when Marcus
finally got the call. But that was still enough time for
a few moments of magic. As soon as he got the ball,
he raced up the left wing, past one defender and

then another.

'Go on, go on!' the fans urged him on. It was now or never for England.

Marcus was into the Iceland box, with Harry Kane and Jamie Vardy waiting in the middle, but a defender slid in and poked the ball away.

'Come on!' Marcus wasn't giving up. He grabbed the ball and raced over to take the corner himself. In those last five minutes, he completed three dangerous dribbles, more than any of his teammates had managed during the rest of the match.

'Why wasn't Rashford on from the start?' the fans were left wondering. Unfortunately, it was all too little too late for England; they were heading home in disgrace.

So, would Marcus's experience at Euro 2016 affect his confidence? Not at all! Two months later, he made his debut for the Under-21s against Norway, and by the final whistle, he was an England hat-trick hero, walking off with the match-ball.

Marcus was simply unstoppable! And he was already looking ahead to the 2018 World Cup.

CHAPTER 16

LEARNING (FROM A LEGEND)

Back at Manchester United, there was great excitement about the new 2016–17 season. They not only had a new star manager – José Mourinho – but also four new star signings:

Defender Eric Bailly,

Midfielder Henrikh Mkhitaryan,

Superstar striker Zlatan Ibrahimović,

And Paul Pogba. He was back! Yes, four years after leaving to join Juventus, Marcus's old teammate from 'The Cage' had returned to Old Trafford.

'This is going to be so good!' Jesse predicted.

And Marcus agreed. Over the summer, he had signed a brand-new contract, and moved from Number

39 to Number 19. He was making real progress, so he
didn't mind about the extra competition in attack.

As much as he loved starting and scoring for
United, Marcus knew that he wasn't ready to be the
club's number-one striker. Not yet, anyway. That was
too much pressure for an eighteen-year-old who had
only recently broken into the first team. But now,
with Zlatan there to partner Wayne and be the team's
top goal scorer, Marcus had time to keep developing
his game.

There was so much to learn from a legend like
'Ibra'. He was one of the best players of all time. Yes,
he could seem a little too confident sometimes, but
he had the talent and determination to back that up
in the big games. He had scored goals everywhere –
at Ajax, Juventus, Inter Milan, Barcelona, PSG – and
had won tons of trophies too.

It was an amazing opportunity for Marcus to
improve as a player and a striker. Each training
session was like being back at school. He watched
Zlatan as carefully as he could and tried to absorb as
much information as possible.

It was Zlatan's mentality and focus that impressed Marcus the most. He had never met anyone who wanted to win as much as Zlatan did. Even in their 'friendly' matches during practice, he charged around the pitch, demanding the ball, and then barking angrily if he didn't get it. He was such a strong character that no-one messed with him, not even Mourinho!

If he ever missed a shot, Zlatan didn't let his head and shoulders drop. No – because he firmly believed that he would score the next one. And off the pitch, he worked so hard to keep himself fit and firing, even in his mid-thirties.

'That's what it takes to stay at the top level,' Zlatan told him one day. 'Especially when José is in charge!'

In the Manchester United first team matches, however, Marcus wasn't getting much game-time at all. He only came on as a second-half sub when United won the Community Shield, and he didn't play at all in their first two Premier League matches.

Oh dear, didn't Mourinho think he was good enough? A new manager was like a new start; Marcus would just have to prove himself all over again.

Away at Hull City, he came off the bench to score a last-minute winner. *GOAL!*

Away at Watford, he played a one-two with Zlatan and then bundled the ball in. *GOAL!*

At home against Leicester City, he converted Juan's cross. *GOAL!*

'That's more like it!' Marcus thought to himself as he raced over to the corner flag to celebrate. No matter what position Mourinho asked him to play, he was going to fight hard for his place in the team.

Marcus had switched from a winger to a striker in the United Under-18s, but now he was back out wide again. The United manager preferred to play Zlatan in the middle, with the other forwards taking it in turns on the wings. Marcus didn't mind, but it did mean that he had more defending to do.

'It's your job to mark the full-back,' Mourinho told him. 'When he goes forward, you track back!'

Sometimes Marcus was on the left and sometimes he was on the right. He had good games and not-so-good games, but they were all part of the learning process. He wasn't giving up or going out on loan; no, he would adapt, and he would succeed. Manchester United was his home and he was growing into a stronger all-round player.

Marcus's biggest problem during those difficult months was goals. From October 2016 through to April 2017, he went twenty Premier League games without scoring at all. The longer his bad run went on, the more people talked about it, and the more pressure he put on himself.

'Nooooo!' Marcus screamed at the sky as he wasted yet another simple chance. He could imagine the frustrated look on his manager's face.

What had happened to his finishing? If he didn't find his scoring touch again soon, Mourinho would have no choice but to drop him.

United made it back to Wembley for the 2017 EFL Cup Final in February, but Marcus spent most of the match on the bench. And when he did come on, he struck his one good chance straight at the Southampton keeper. Noooo! It was the same old story, with Zlatan saving the day for United instead.

Marcus was pleased to pick up another winner's
medal, but he didn't feel like he fully deserved it.
He had lost his magic touch! Oh well, he just had
to stay strong and keep believing; that's what he'd
learnt from Ibra. This was just another obstacle that
he had to overcome.

Away at Sunderland, Marcus came on for Jesse
with half an hour to go. United were already 2–0
up against the team in twentieth place. Surely, he
wouldn't get a better chance to end his goal drought.

But before he knew it, they were into the last
five minutes and Marcus still hadn't even had a
shot. 'Noooooooooo!' Was he going to go yet another
league game without a goal?

In the very last minute, he raced down the right
wing and then passed inside to Zlatan. He thought
about shooting himself, but instead, he slipped it
back to Marcus, who was now into the penalty area.
This was it – his big moment to score.

'Go back to basics' – that's what everyone had told
him to do: Zlatan, Mourinho, Wayne, Giggsy. 'Just
pick a spot and shoot.' Marcus kept his cool, even as

the Sunderland defender slid in to try and tackle him. *BANG!* His shot flew past Jordan Pickford and into the bottom corner.

Gooooooooooooooooooooaaaaaaaaaaaaaaaaalllllllllllll llllllllllllll!!!!!!!!!!!!!!!!!!!!!

As he got up off the grass, Marcus threw his arms high into the air. Yes, another Premier League goal at last!

'Thanks for passing!' he shouted to Zlatan as they shared a high-five.

'No problem, you needed that. Now you've just got to keep on scoring!'

Zlatan's wise words became even more important a few weeks later, when he injured his knee in the Europa League. Could Marcus step up and be United's match-winner instead?

CHAPTER 17

EUROPEAN GLORY

'Arghhhh!' Zlatan cried out as he collapsed onto the grass in agony.

It was 1–1 in the ninetieth minute of United's Europa League quarter-final second leg against the Belgian club, Anderlecht, and their star striker had just picked up a horrible injury.

After jumping up to win the ball, Zlatan had landed awkwardly, twisting his right knee. Everyone knew that he wasn't the kind of guy who went down easily. Uh oh, what were United going to do without him?

Marcus was already on the pitch, playing on the left wing, but Mourinho decided to move him into the middle. This was his chance to show that he was a top striker who could take over from Zlatan.

'Come on!' the United fans urged him on.

Despite his struggles in the Premier League, Marcus was enjoying a good spell in the Europa League. After all, that was where his United career had started, with those two goals against FC Midtjylland. He loved the competition.

Under Mourinho, Marcus wasn't scoring so often, but he was getting better and better at setting up goals for others:

One for Zlatan against Saint-Étienne,

One for Henrikh in the first leg against Anderlecht,

And another for Henrikh earlier on in the second leg.

He was creating lots of chances for his teammates, but now Marcus needed to be United's main striker. His job in extra-time was to shoot his team into the Europa League semi-finals.

'I can do this,' he told himself, as calm and focused as ever. He knew that he would have to do a lot better than his earlier efforts in the game:

A long-range strike that he dragged well wide,

A left-foot shot that hit the side netting,

And a one-on-one where he took the ball around the keeper, but his touch was too heavy.

'Noooooooooo!' Marcus screamed out in frustration. What was going on? He was normally so good at one-on-ones.

Marcus had to find his shooting boots again, and quickly. Otherwise, United would be out.

Early in the second half of extra-time, Marouane headed the ball down to Marcus just inside the crowded Anderlecht penalty area. What an opportunity! His first touch was beautiful to bring it under control, and his second was even better.

Just as a defender dived in for the block, Marcus dragged the ball back. Cruyff Turn! He was on his weaker left foot now and a little off-balance too, but he still knew exactly where the bottom corner was.

Goooooooooooooooooooooaaaaaaaaaaaaaaaallllllllllll llllllllllllllll!!!!!!!!!!!!!!!!!!!!!

It wasn't one of Marcus's best strikes, but it was certainly one of his most important goals. When his team needed him most, he had delivered. United were only thirteen minutes away from the semi-finals now. Looking up at the fans, he leapt high into the air, his fists clenched with passion.

'Come onnnnnnn!' he roared.

Sadly, Zlatan's season was over, which meant that Marcus was now Manchester United's first-choice striker. So, could he lead his club to the Europa League final? Yes!

'Keep a clean sheet and try to get an away goal.' That was Mourinho's plan for the first leg against Celta Vigo. The defence stayed strong, and Marcus did the rest. In the twentieth minute, he curled a powerful shot towards the top corner, but the keeper tipped it past the post. So close!

There was nothing that the keeper could do to stop Marcus's fantastic free kick in the second half, however. From wide on the right, it looked like Daley Blind would cross it in with his left foot, but instead, he dummied it for Marcus. United's striker had won the free kick in the first place, and now he was going to take it himself. With a whip of his right foot, he sent the ball swerving into the far corner of the net. 1–0!

*Goooooooooooooooooooaaaaaaaaaaaaaaaalllllllllllll
lllllllllllllll!!!!!!!!!!!!!!!!!!!!!*

Job done! And back at Old Trafford, Marcus made
sure of the victory with another moment of magic.
From the left wing, he swung in a perfect cross for
Marouane to head home at the back post. It was 2–0
– and United were into the Europa League Final!

'And we're going to win it!' Marcus and Paul
celebrated together.

Their opponents in Athens would be Ajax, one
of the best young teams in the world. They had
Davinson Sánchez and Matthijs de Ligt at the back,
Hakim Ziyech and Davy Klaassen in midfield, and
Kasper Dolberg in attack.

United certainly had a lot more experience in their
line-up, plus one of the most exciting young strikers
on the planet.

Marcus wasn't fazed by a big European final. He
had already won twice at Wembley and also played for
England at the Euros. So as the two teams walked out
onto the pitch, he looked as calmly confident as ever.

United were going to win, and they were
determined to win it for Manchester. Just two days
earlier, twenty-two people had tragically died following
a terrorist attack at an Ariana Grande concert in the
city. The local people were still shocked and distraught,
but Marcus and his teammates would do their best to
bring them back a bit of joy, and a trophy too.

In the sixteenth minute of the game, Marcus
played a neat one-two with Juan on the edge of the
Ajax box. Patiently, they worked the ball across to
Marouane and finally to Paul. *BANG!* His shot took
a big deflection off Sánchez, giving the keeper no
chance of stopping it. *1–0!*

'Yessss!' Marcus cried out, racing over to celebrate
with Paul.

Early in the second half, Henrikh scored a second
goal, and Ajax couldn't come back from that. United
were the new Europa League Champions! And to
make things even better, they would now be playing
in the Champions League next season.

'Hurraaaaaaaay!' Marcus hadn't been the hero this
time, but he had worked really hard for his team,

up front on his own; making runs, battling for the ball, and causing lots of problems for the Ajax centre-backs. This time, in the final, he had definitely played his part.

At the final whistle, Marcus had hugs for everyone: Henrikh, Juan, Jesse, Paul, Daley, Michael, Marouane, his old academy mate Axel… And Zlatan, who had come all the way to Greece to cheer his teammates on to European glory.

'Great game, great win!' he congratulated Marcus.

Later that night, United's two top strikers posed for a photo together with the trophy. On one side, a football legend; on the other, a future superstar.

CHAPTER 18

NEW SEASON, SAME POSITION

With Zlatan out injured for at least another six months, would Marcus be Manchester United's main striker for the start of the 2017–18 season? He looked taller, stronger and better than ever when he returned for pre-season training. He now felt ready for the extra responsibility.

But despite Marcus's key role in their Europa League glory, Mourinho had a different plan. In order to compete for the Premier League title, he wanted a big, reliable, goalscoring Number 9, not an inconsistent but talented teenager who was still growing. So United signed Romelu Lukaku from Everton for £75 million.

For Marcus, that meant new season, same position – left wing. Oh well – it didn't matter where he played, just as long as he played. And played well.

Marcus dribbled forward at full speed from deep in his own half, bursting into the space behind the West Ham right-back. In a flash, he was almost on the edge of the penalty area…

'Yes!' Romelu called for it, pointing towards the gap between the centre-backs. Marcus knew exactly what kind of pass a striker would want. He delivered the perfect through-ball for United's new Number 9 to strike first time. *1–0!*

As he raced away to celebrate, Romelu pointed again, this time at Marcus. 'What a ball!' he cried out, thanking him with a bear hug.

Marcus was happy to help his teammates, but he preferred getting the goals himself. Nothing could beat that buzz. He scored:

One against Leicester City,

One against Stoke City,

One against Basel on his Champions League debut,

And two against Burton Albion in the EFL Cup.

Five goals in five games! It was so far so good for the new season.

With United competing for four trophies, Marcus couldn't play every minute of every match. But whether he started the game, or came on as a super sub, he always did his best to make an impact. He celebrated his twentieth birthday by coming off the bench in the Champions League against Benfica.

'Over here, Rom – pass it!'

After only one minute on the pitch, Marcus was already on the attack, sprinting past the right-back and into the Benfica box. He twisted and turned his way past one defender, then tried to squeeze his way in between two more, until eventually they fouled him. Penalty!

'Nice run, Rash!' Romelu said, helping him back up to his feet.

Marcus was now up to seven goals and five assists for the season, and November hadn't even started yet!

By January, however, his great form had faded, and he found himself back on the bench again. Even when Mourinho gave Romelu a rest, it was Anthony who played up front instead.

And on the left wing? Well, United had just signed Alexis Sánchez from Arsenal. So at most, Marcus was getting fifteen minutes at the end of matches to try to create some magic.

'Now I'm never going to get my form back!' he told his brothers miserably. He needed the rhythm of regular game-time to get his season back on track.

'Hey, just keep working hard,' they tried to reassure him. 'And be patient – remember, you're only twenty!'

Marcus nodded. It was easy to forget sometimes just how young he still was. But by February, he was hardly playing for United. Sometimes, he wasn't even in Mourinho's matchday squad at all.

'Where's Rashford?' the fans wondered when they looked at the team sheet against Newcastle. 'Is he injured?'

It was a tough time for Marcus, but he didn't give up. He was too determined for that. All he needed was one more opportunity…

Away at Crystal Palace in early March, United

were 1–0 down at half-time. What was Mourinho going to do now? Romelu, Jesse and Alexis were already on the pitch, and Anthony was out injured… So the manager took off a midfielder and brought on Marcus.

Wow, a whole forty-five minutes! But things actually got worse before they got better. Early in the second half, Palace scored again from a quick free kick. *2–0!*

Uh oh. United really needed a gamechanger now. Although Marcus didn't get a goal or an assist, he helped to turn things around. With his positive forward runs, he pushed his team further and further up the pitch, in search of goals.

Chris Smalling headed in the first, then Romelu equalised, then Nemanja scored a screamer. What an incredible comeback: 3–2 to United!

After that, Mourinho simply *had* to start Marcus in the next league match: at home against Liverpool. It was one of the biggest rivalries in British football, and a game that United always had to win. But how? Playing on the left wing, Marcus would be up against

Trent Alexander-Arnold, a young right-back who was known for his attacking, rather than his defending.

'Use your speed to get in behind him,' Mourinho told Marcus. 'Go out there and give him the hardest game of his young career!'

'Yes, Boss!'

In the fourteenth minute, David sent a long goal-kick upfield towards Romelu. As he jumped for the ball with Dejan Lovren, Marcus was already on the move behind him, hoping for the flick-on. By the time that Alexander-Arnold saw the danger, it was already too late for Liverpool.

ZOOM! Marcus burst into the box, Cruyff-turned his way onto his right foot and,

BANG! He fired a shot into the far corner. *1–0!*

Gooooooooooooooooooooaaaaaaaaaaaaaaaalllllllllllll llllllllllllllll!!!!!!!!!!!!!!!!!!!

As Old Trafford went wild all around him, Marcus raced over to celebrate with the fans. He was one of them, after all.

'Yes Rash, what a strike!' Ashley Young yelled, wrapping him in a tight hug.

Ten minutes later, Marcus did it again. This time, as Romelu and Alexis attacked through the middle, he stayed out wide on the left. Virgil van Dijk eventually tackled Alexis, but the ball bounced out to the edge of the area...

Alexander-Arnold had chased back to help the other defenders, leaving Marcus all alone with the ball travelling towards him. He didn't think; he just hit it, low into the far corner again. *2–0!*

Goooooooooooooooooooooaaaaaaaaaaaaaaaaalllllllllllll llllllllllllll!!!!!!!!!!!!!!!!!!!

With his arms outstretched, Marcus stood by the corner flag and soaked up all the cheers and applause. What a feeling! Scoring two goals against Liverpool was enough to make you a Manchester United hero for life.

The overall season would go down as a disappointing one for Marcus, but with performances like that one, his time would definitely come soon.

CHAPTER 19

2018 WORLD CUP

Gareth Southgate announced his England squad
for the 2018 World Cup with a special video,
where each player's name was revealed one by
one. Raheem Sterling was first, then John Stones,
then Trent Alexander-Arnold...

Eventually, two kids appeared on screen, standing
in a Manchester street. One was wearing a red
England shirt and he turned around to show the
name on the back:

'Marcus... RASHFORD!' they cheered together.
'The boy wonder.'

His Euro 2016 call-up had been a total shock,
but Marcus wasn't surprised to be in the 2018

126

World Cup squad. He had been playing well for his country for a while now. Even so, it was an amazing moment, and another childhood dream come true.

'After years of you standing on the touch line in the cold and rain, Mum we're off to the World Cup!' he tweeted with a picture of Melanie looking proud.

Marcus had been busy training with United on the morning of the big announcement, but he returned home to find lots of nice messages from his friends and family. He tried to play it cool like usual, but inside he was buzzing with excitement.

'Russia, here we come!' he messaged Jesse.

Would they return home as World Cup heroes? Ahead of the tournament, Southgate had switched the formation from a 4–3–3 to a 3–5–2 with wing-backs. It meant one more player in midfield, and one less player in attack.

That was good news for Jesse, and bad news for Marcus. Harry and Raheem were England's first-choice forwards, but hopefully he could come on and be the super sub. If the team needed someone to make an impact off the bench, then he would be ready and waiting.

Marcus sent out a final 'Pick me!' to Southgate in the team's last friendly against Costa Rica. In the thirteenth minute, he got the ball on the right, with time and space to think. What next? In a flash, he spotted that the keeper had come forward a little, off his goal line.

Some players might have seen it and thought, 'No, not worth trying', but Marcus was confident enough to give anything a go. *BANG!* Before the poor keeper knew what was going on, the ball was dipping and swerving over his head… and into the far corner of the net. *1–0!*

Goooooooooooooooooooooaaaaaaaaaaaaaaaallllllllllllll llllllllllllll!!!!!!!!!!!!!!!!!!!!

It was one of his best strikes ever, but Marcus didn't show any emotion. He just threw his arms out and walked away, as if he did that every day. Yes, if England needed a moment of World Cup magic, he would be ready and waiting.

In the first match in Volgograd, against Tunisia, it didn't look like they'd need Marcus at all. Harry scored an early goal and England were cruising, but out of nowhere, Tunisia scored a penalty. Suddenly it was 1–1, and a draw wouldn't do for England.

In the sixty-eighth minute, Marcus came on for Raheem. On his World Cup debut, what could he do to help his country?

'Our passing's too slow,' he signalled to his teammates. 'We've got to move it around more quickly!'

Marcus ran and ran, desperate to do something special. It was only in the final five minutes, however, that he was able to get himself on the ball and into the game. With a burst of speed, he dribbled down the right wing and won another corner for England.

Come on!

Seconds later, as Ruben Loftus-Cheek cut the ball back, Marcus was in space near the penalty spot. Perfect! This was it: his chance to score the winner. But then…

'Leave it!' he heard Jesse shout at the last second.

But when Marcus dummied it, the ball got stuck under Jesse's feet.

'Nooooooo!' Marcus snarled, turning away in anger.

Thankfully, Harry scored a last-minute header to give England the victory. Phew!

'In our first game, it's just good to get the three points,' Marcus told the media afterwards, sounding so mature for his age. 'Now we can relax our way into the tournament.'

In their second group match, even without Marcus on the pitch, England thrashed Panama 6–1. Although he was sad to miss out on such a goal-fest, he did get to start the next match against Marouane's Belgium.

Both nations were already through to the Round of 16, and so the managers rested their stars. But for squad players like Marcus, it was a massive opportunity. Raheem had now gone twenty-two games without a goal for England. Many fans were already calling for Marcus to play instead, so if he could score against Belgium…

Sadly, Marcus failed to take the few chances he got. He curled his first shot way past the post and then missed a crucial one-on-one against Thibaut Courtois.

'Come on, you've got to do better than that!' he shouted at himself.

England lost 1–0, Belgium won the group, and Marcus moved back to the bench. His World Cup, however, wasn't over yet.

In the Round of 16 against Colombia, Southgate brought Marcus on as England's fourth substitute, deep in extra-time. There was one obvious reason for that: PENALTIES! Yes, it looked like they were heading for another horrible shoot-out, and for that, England would need their coolest, calmest players on the pitch.

Nothing fazed Marcus; he was totally fearless. But as he walked forward to take England's second spot-kick, all three penalties so far had been scored. The pressure was on.

'Go on, Rash!' Jordan shouted as he threw the ball to him.

With quick, confident strides, Marcus entered the penalty area and placed it down carefully on the spot. As he stepped back to start his run-up, he fixed his eyes first on the ball and then on the goal in front of him. That helped him to focus and ignore the noise of the crowd.

After four little shuffles to the left, Marcus moved forward, taking short steps to try to fool the keeper. David Ospina did guess the right way, but Marcus tucked the ball right into the bottom corner. *GOAL!*

Ice-cold! He didn't celebrate at all; not even a fist pump. Instead, Marcus jogged over to Jordan to give him some encouragement. It worked. Six spot-kicks later, England had won the shoot-out. They were into the World Cup quarter-finals!

'Yesssssssssss!' Marcus didn't join the big player pile-up, but he stood next to it, smiling. What a moment, what an achievement! He was so proud to be a part of English football history.

And their Russian adventure continued. The quarter-final finished England 2 Sweden 0. Easy! Marcus had only come on for the last minute, but winning was one big squad effort. Everyone could see that, especially the fans back home. They had fallen in love with the national team again.

There were high hopes for the semi-final against

Croatia and it started so well. In the fifth minute,
Kieran Trippier curled a free kick into the top corner.
1–0!

'Get in!' Marcus punched the air on the sidelines.

But in the second half, as England tired, Croatia
seemed to grow stronger. With twenty minutes to go,
Ivan Perišić got the equaliser. *1–1!*

'Marcus, get ready – you're coming on!'

'Yes, Coach!'

With his fast, fresh legs, Marcus was determined
to make an impact. He chased after every long punt
and pass, putting the Croatian defenders under
pressure. If only he could get one good chance...

As the ball dropped, Domagoj Vida missed his
header and for a second, it looked like Marcus might
be in. But it bounced up over his head and the
Croatian keeper rushed out to collect it.

'Ohhhhhhhhh!' groaned every England player and
supporter, including Marcus.

He kept chasing everything right until the end
of extra-time, but by then, Croatia had scored the
winning goal. It was all over, and England were out

of the World Cup.

At the final whistle, Marcus collapsed onto the grass, his hands covering the tears streaming down his face. It was a devastating feeling, one of the worst he had ever experienced. He had given absolutely everything, and yet it hadn't been enough.

'Hey, you've been brilliant,' Southgate said, helping him back up. 'You should be so proud of what you've achieved!'

Although his manager was right, it didn't feel that way out there on the pitch in Moscow. It was so disappointing to come so close. As the players stood in front of the fans, thanking them for all their support, Marcus was already thinking ahead to next time.

Next time, he would be starring in the starting line-up.

And next time, he would lead England all the way to the World Cup final.

CHAPTER 20

UNITED'S NEW NUMBER 10

Marcus returned from the 2018 World Cup feeling more determined than ever. He was going to make this his greatest year yet at Old Trafford, the season where he went from inconsistent kid to reliable scorer, from 'Boy Wonder' to 'Star Striker'. It was time. Marcus was nearly twenty-one now, and he was also United's new Number 10.

Wow, what an honour! That shirt had been worn by so many of the club's most famous forwards:

Denis Law,

Mark Hughes,

Teddy Sheringham,

Ruud van Nistelrooy,

And, of course, Wayne Rooney, his hero and mentor.

'It suits you mate,' he wrote on social media when Marcus first wore his old number.

It was one of his proudest moments, especially as a lifelong Manchester United fan. Now, Marcus had to prove himself worthy to wear the shirt. He had scored seven Premier League goals last season and now he was looking to double that, at least.

'Let's do this!' he said with one arm around Romelu and the other around Anthony. They were Numbers 9, 10 and 11 now and between them, they had everything they needed to become one of the best attacking trios in Europe.

The new season didn't start the way Marcus had hoped, however. After a win against Leicester, they lost to Brighton and then, things would get even worse against Burnley, despite a promising start: United were already winning 2–0 when he came on. It should have been a nice, comfortable afternoon, but instead, he surprisingly lost his cool.

As Marcus tried to dribble past Phil Bardsley, the

Burnley right-back kicked the ball out for a corner
and then took a second, angry kick at him.

'Hey!' Marcus cried out as he fell to the floor.
'You can't do that!'

When he got back up, Marcus walked over
towards Bardsley. He was so furious that he made
the mistake of going head-to-head with the defender.

'Ref!' Bardsley called out, touching his head and
pretending to be in pain. 'Did you see that?'

The referee ran over and reached into his pocket:
RED CARD!

What? Marcus couldn't believe it. At first, he
blamed Bardsley and the referee, but once he had
calmed down a bit in the dressing room, he realised
it was really his own fault. How could he be so
stupid? He had fallen for the oldest trick in the book!

'Sorry to everyone at the club and all the fans,'
Marcus wrote on Twitter. He had learnt his lesson.

After that bad start to a fresh chapter as United's
new Number 10, Marcus soon bounced back. He
wasn't yet banging in the goals every game, but he
showed flashes of his brilliance. He scored a flick

volley against West Ham, he caught the Fulham keeper out at his near post, and he grabbed a last-minute winner away at Bournemouth.

'Come on!' Marcus roared as he raced over to the United fans in the corner. That was more like it; he was scoring goals when his team needed him most.

Although it was an important win, there was still plenty of room for improvement. United were meant to be challenging for the Premier League title, or at least the Top Four, but instead, they were way down in eighth place. That simply wasn't good enough, especially with such a talented and expensive squad.

'We spent £90 million on Pogba – what a waste of money that was!' some supporters moaned. 'And what's happened to Rashford? I thought he was going to be as good as Mbappé!'

All was not well at Old Trafford. In December, the club directors decided that it was time for another fresh start. They were going to replace Mourinho with a new manager, and announced that, until the end of the season, that would be Ole Gunnar Solskjær, the legendary striker who had scored United's winning goal in the 1999 Champions League final.

The atmosphere at the club seemed to change straight away. Suddenly, everyone was excited again:

Ole's at the wheel,
Tell me how does it feel,
We've got Sanchez, Paul Pogba and Fred,
Marcus Rashford, a Manc born and bred,
Duh du, du du du du du
Duh du, du du du du du!

Solskjær was certainly a fans' favourite, but could he really help to turn things around at Old Trafford? As a fellow striker, Marcus had a good feeling about it.

CHAPTER 21

SCORING AGAIN UNDER SOLSKJÆR

Solskjær's first message to the Manchester United players was clear and simple: 'I want us to play forward and I was us to play fast.'

After all, what was the point in having the power of Paul and the pace of Marcus and Anthony in attack if they weren't going to use it properly? The plan was to bring back the style of the United of old, the one that had won so many trophies under Sir Alex Ferguson. That team had been impossible to stop, and also exciting to watch.

'Yeah!' everyone agreed eagerly.

There was lots of work to be done first, however, all over the pitch. As a former striker himself,

Solskjær focused on helping the forwards in particular. He could understand Marcus's amazing potential – his speed, his skill, his strength, his intelligence – but he could also see the weaknesses in his game.

'I want you to be our star striker from now on,' the manager encouraged him. 'I know you can do it, but you need to score more goals. So let's turn you into a clinical finisher!'

Together, they worked hard on Marcus's movement in the box and, most importantly, his composure in front of goal.

'Don't rush the shot!' Solskjær kept telling him. 'Take your time, stay calm and pick your spot. The goal's not going to move!'

Soon, Marcus was ready to put that finishing into practice on the pitch. Meanwhile, Solskjær continued to assemble his squad for his first match as United manager. He picked:

Anthony on the left,

Jesse on the right,

And Marcus in the middle!

Marcus knew his new manager really believed in him, and that gave him a much-needed boost. Now, it was time to say thanks.

In the second minute of the away match against Cardiff City, the opposition gave away a free kick just outside their penalty area. And up stepped Marcus to blast the ball into the bottom corner. *1–0!*

Gooooooooooooooooooooaaaaaaaaaaaaaaaaalllllllllllll lllllllllllllll!!!!!!!!!!!!!!!!!!!!

At the full-time whistle, United were 5–1 winners. What a start!

Marcus was delighted to score another fantastic free kick, but he kept thinking about the one-on-one that he had missed in the second half. Despite staying calm and picking his spot, the Cardiff keeper had deflected his shot wide. Had Marcus rushed his finish again? Should he have aimed for the other side instead?

'Hey, don't worry about it,' Solskjær reassured him. 'You'll score that next time.'

Marcus was a man on a mission. In the fourth minute against Bournemouth, he danced his way through their defence with Ronaldo-esque footwork.

He poked the ball past the first, then did an elástico to escape from the second, before crossing it for Paul to tap in. 1–0!

Marcus had an assist; now he wanted a goal of his own. At the end of the first half, Anthony delivered a deep cross towards the Bournemouth back post. With a burst of speed, Marcus got to it first, stretched out his right boot, and somehow flicked the ball into the opposite corner of the net. *3–0!*

Goooooooooooooooooooooaaaaaaaaaaaaaaaaalllllllllllll llllllllllllllll!!!!!!!!!!!!!!!!!!!!!

With Solskjær's support, Marcus was back to his absolute best, and it was beautiful to watch. He was playing almost every minute of every United match.

Away at Newcastle, Alexis passed it through to Marcus, who was unmarked on the edge of the six-yard box. It was one of those chances that a star striker simply had to score. As the keeper rushed out towards him, Marcus took one touch to control the ball and then calmly placed it past Martin Dúbravka. *2–0!*

Goooooooooooooooooooooaaaaaaaaaaaaaaaaalllllllllllll llllllllllllllll!!!!!!!!!!!!!!!!!!!!!

On the sidelines, Solskjær clapped and smiled.
Much better, Marcus!

'He's got frightening pace, he's now become
stronger, he can hold the ball up for us and he's a
great link player,' the United manager told the media.
'He can become a top, top player.'

Now that Marcus had finally found his striker's
rhythm, the goals were flooding in.

Away at Tottenham, Paul spotted Marcus's run
and played the perfect long pass. As he reached the
ball on the edge of the penalty area, Marcus thought
about hitting it first time, but then he heard his
manager's voice in his head:

'Don't rush the shot!'

So instead, he took a touch and carefully picked
his spot. *BANG!* – bottom corner. *1–0!*

*Goooooooooooooooooooooaaaaaaaaaaaaaaaaalllllllllllll
llllllllllllll!!!!!!!!!!!!!!!!!!!!*

It was a brilliant strike from a very difficult angle,
but Marcus made it look so easy. His finishing was
improving with every game and every goal.

'Come on!' he shouted, punching the air with

passion. He was getting used to that great goalscoring feeling. He scored the winners for United against Brighton and Leicester City too.

Six goals in eight games! That took him up to nine for the Premier League season, his best-ever total. At last, this was the big breakthrough that Marcus had been working towards; his move from 'Boy Wonder' to 'Star Striker'.

One of his old teammates agreed: 'Rashford is the future of Manchester United,' Zlatan announced. 'Now he is using his quality more for the team, not just for himself. He has big potential – he has no limits.'

In the Champions League, Marcus came face-to-face with Europe's top wonderkid, Kylian Mbappé. Let the battle begin! The Frenchman won the first leg, scoring PSG's second goal at Old Trafford, but it was Marcus who won the second leg in Paris.

First, he hit a long-range rocket that Gianluigi Buffon couldn't hold. Romelu raced in to grab the rebound. *GOAL!*

'Come on, we can do this!' Marcus cheered with confidence.

Then, in the very last minute, just when it looked like it was all over for United, they won a penalty. And after four long minutes of VAR and arguing, it was Marcus who stepped up to take it. It was the biggest moment of his football career, but he was a calm, clinical, world-class finisher now.

Goooooooooooooooooooooaaaaaaaaaaaaaaaalllllllllllll lllllllllllllll!!!!!!!!!!!!!!!!!!!!

'Yes, Rash!'

'What a hero!' his teammates cheered as they chased him over to the corner flag.

United were through to the Champions League quarter-finals, thanks to their new star striker.

Unfortunately, their form soon fizzled out after that, but for Marcus, the most important thing was making progress. As a team, they were starting to play more exciting football, and as a striker, he was starting to look like a more lethal finisher. 2018–19 had been his best scoring season so far, and 2019–20 was going to be even better.

CHAPTER 22

FINDING THE NET IN THE NATIONS LEAGUE

Marcus was starting to get more game-time for England too. After the 2018 World Cup, Southgate decided to switch formation again, this time back to a 4–3–3. Suddenly, there was space for three forwards in the team: Raheem, Harry and one more... Marcus!

Although he was the most popular choice, there was plenty of competition: Danny Welbeck, James Maddison, Callum Wilson, and Jadon Sancho, the new boy wonder on the block. Jadon was only eighteen and he was already playing brilliantly on the right wing for Borussia Dortmund in Germany.

'Man, you're making me feel old!' Marcus joked.

He knew that he would need to work hard to secure that starting spot, starting with the UEFA Nations League. It was a brand-new European tournament and England were up against two of the top teams in the world: Spain and their World Cup rivals, Croatia. Wow, it wouldn't be easy, but Marcus always loved a challenge.

'They're going to be really good games for us,' he said in an interview. 'We have to start beating these bigger countries in the world and there's no two better opponents to do that against.'

In order to win, England would need goals, and not just from Harry. So far, Marcus had only scored three international goals in twenty-five appearances. Okay, so he had come off the bench in a lot of those games, but still, it was a disappointing record for someone who was supposed to be a striker. It was time to change that.

At Wembley, England got off to the perfect start against Spain. As Harry spread the ball out to Luke Shaw on the left, Marcus was already in position, between the defenders, and ready to make his move.

'Now!' he called out, bursting into the box.

Luke's pass was perfect and so was Marcus's finish, past their United teammate, David. *1–0!*

Goooooooooooooooooooaaaaaaaaaaaaaaaaaalllllllllllll llllllllllllllll!!!!!!!!!!!!!!!!!!!!!!

Marcus didn't race away to celebrate; he jogged. He was Mr Cool, especially in front of goal these days. For United, and now for England too.

Sadly, Spain fought back to win 2–1, but Marcus knew that the team was moving in the right direction. He certainly was. Three days later, in a friendly against Switzerland, he snuck in at the back post to volley home the winner.

'What a finish, Rash!' Danny Rose shouted, giving him a big hug.

Two in two – England had a new star striker now!

Marcus missed a couple of good chances in the disappointing 0–0 draw against Croatia, but he didn't let that get him down. Instead, he looked forward, to England's second game against Spain. It was now a must-win match. Otherwise, they had no chance of making it to the Nations League Finals.

'Come on, we can do this!' Southgate told his team before kick-off.

For Marcus, it felt like a massive moment in his international career. If he failed, Jadon was there, waiting impatiently on the bench, ready to take his place. But if he succeeded…

For the first forty magnificent minutes, England's exciting new front three destroyed the Spanish defence together.

First, Harry passed to Marcus, who delivered a dangerous cross to Raheem. *1–0!*

Then Harry slipped a brilliant pass through to Marcus, who calmly fired a shot into the bottom corner. *2–0!*

And finally, Harry slid the ball across to Raheem in the six-yard box. *3–0!*

'Yesssss!' Marcus punched the air with pride. The England attack was on fire, and they were having so much fun together. Their speed, their skill, their movement and their shooting; they were too hot for even top defenders like Sergio Ramos to handle.

Although Spain fought back in the second half

once again, this time, England held on for a huge
3–2 victory.

'Top work tonight!' Southgate told Marcus with a
smile and hug as the squad celebrated out on the pitch.

'Thanks, Boss!'

Hopefully, with more goals and more performances
like that, Marcus could secure his place alongside
Raheem and Harry in attack.

'Rashford is a tremendous talent,' Southgate
confirmed, just in case anyone still doubted it.

With a 2–1 win over Croatia, England made it
through to the Nations League Finals, where they
faced the Netherlands in the semis. Harry was out
injured, so Marcus was now England's central striker,
up against two of the best defenders in the world:
Virgil van Dijk and Matthijs de Ligt.

'Bring it on!' Marcus had given de Ligt a tough
game in the Europa League final back in 2017; now,
it was time to test him again.

In the thirtieth minute, the Netherlands were
looking very comfortable as they passed the ball
around at the back. But as it came to de Ligt, he lost

his concentration and let it slip under his foot. It was only a half-mistake, but that was all that Marcus needed. In a sprint race, he could beat almost anyone. He got to the ball first, just before de Ligt, who kicked Marcus's shin instead. *Penalty!*

He picked himself up and put the ball down on the spot. Without Harry, Marcus was England's penalty taker now. No problem! After four little shuffles to the left, he moved forward, taking short steps to try to fool the keeper. It worked. As Jasper Cillessen dived to his right, Marcus placed his shot in the opposite corner. *1–0!*

Goooooooooooooooooooooaaaaaaaaaaaaaaaaaalllllllllllll llllllllllllll!!!!!!!!!!!!!!!!!!!

As cool as you like! He jogged over to the England fans, holding up the Three Lions on his shirt. Harry who? Marcus was a top finisher too!

When the second half started, however, he wasn't out there on the pitch. Marcus had tried his best to ignore his injured ankle, but eventually, it was just too painful to play on.

'Good luck, lads!' he told his teammates.

Without Marcus, however, England lost their way. From 1–0 up, they fell to a 3–1 defeat and crashed out of the competition.

It was a disappointing way to end, but overall, Marcus had enjoyed his first Nations League experience. Hopefully his three goals had earned him a regular England starting spot, especially with the next Euros coming up soon.

CHAPTER 23

UNITED'S STAR STRIKER

30 October 2019, Stamford Bridge, London

Almost three months into the new season, and Manchester United were still struggling to find their form. Their new star striker, however, had certainly found his. Marcus's scoring run had started on the opening day with two classy finishes against Chelsea. Now, United were on their way to Stamford Bridge to take on Chelsea again, this time in the Carabao Cup fourth round.

As the team travelled down to London, Marcus had every reason to feel confident. It had been a fantastic week for him. First, he had converted

Daniel James' cross to end Liverpool's seventeen-match winning streak, and then he had calmly slotted home against Norwich City. That was his fifth goal of the season and his fiftieth for United.

Two in two! Even a missed penalty wasn't going to get him down. Harry Kane, Sergio Agüero, Pierre-Emerick Aubameyang, and Marcus Rashford – *that's* where he was aiming to be, amongst the most prolific strikers in the Premier League.

'Yes!' Marcus called out for the ball, as Daniel dribbled up the right wing. He was in space on the edge of the area, in between two Chelsea defenders. Daniel, however, decided to go it alone. He danced his way into the box, where Marcos Alonso brought him down. *Penalty to United!*

'Great work!' Marcus told Daniel, quickly grabbing the ball. He was determined to take it, despite that miss against Norwich.

Marcus went through his usual spot-kick routine, but faster this time, as if he couldn't wait to…

SCORE! *1–0!*

Goooooooooooooaaaaaaaaaaaalllllllllllllllllll!!!!!!!!!!!!!!!

It was a perfect penalty, sending the keeper the wrong way. As Marcus and his teammates celebrated with cool high-fives, their manager, Solskjær, punched the air with both fists. Thank goodness their star striker was on fire!

United's lead lasted all the way until the sixtieth minute, when Michy Batshuayi scored a superb solo goal. 1–1! Uh oh, the pressure was back on the team in red. They needed something special from their star striker, otherwise their cup run would be over.

In the seventy-second minute, Fred won a free kick for United, thirty-five yards out from the Chelsea goal. It would take a wonderstrike to beat Willy Caballero from there, but Marcus was always up for a challenge.

Although he was getting better and better at scoring tap-ins these days, he still preferred the spectacular long-range rockets he hit like those of Cristiano Ronaldo. Those were the shots that Marcus practised most after training, and they were the goals that he remembered most too. That free kick against Celta Vigo in the Europa League semi-final, that dipping, swerving shot for England versus Costa Rica; those were moments that Marcus would never ever forget.

It was time to add one more to that incredible collection, on the night before his twenty-second birthday. One, two, three steps and then BANG! As soon as the ball left his boot, Marcus knew that it was a good, clean strike. He watched it fly high over the jumping heads in the Chelsea wall…

'Now, down and a little to the left!' Marcus muttered, as if the ball could hear him.

Maybe it could because not only did it dip, but it also swerved, away from Caballero and into the top corner. 2–1!

Goooooooooooooooooooooaaaaaaaaaaaaaaaallllllllllllllllll llllllllllll!!!!!!!!!!!!!!!!!!!!!

It was a beauty, easily one of the best he had ever scored. What a way to win a match! Marcus raced away to celebrate, sliding on his knees towards the United fans in the corner.

'You hero!' Ashley screamed, hugging him tightly as he got back up to his feet.

'Come on!' Marcus roared over his teammate's shoulder.

There was nothing he loved more than scoring spectacular strikes for his club. Like his hero Cristiano, he was now combining skills with goals. Marcus was so proud to be United's new Number 10, their consistent star striker at last.

After that stunner at Stamford Bridge, the goals kept coming. Now that he had found his rhythm, suddenly Marcus just couldn't stop scoring: against Partizan Belgrade in the Europe League; then back in the Premier League against Brighton, Sheffield United, two against Tottenham, and then one in United's Manchester derby win over City.

Marcus didn't even have to think about it anymore; he just shot and scored. Simple!

He grabbed one against Colchester in the Carabao Cup quarter-finals, then one against Newcastle, one against Burnley, and another two against Norwich.

Wow, it was still only January, and Marcus was already up to nineteen goals for the season! He had well and truly smashed all of his previous scoring records.

'Rashford is really starting to look like the real deal,' one journalist wrote. 'He now deserves to be called world class.'

Nearly four years after his dream debut against FC Midtjylland, Marcus was at last living up to those early expectations. There had been tough times along the way, but he had never stopped believing in himself and his ability. Now, it was official; the boy wonder had become United's star striker.

And a few months later, Marcus made another massive leap, this time from football hero to national hero. Despite all the fame and fortune of playing for Manchester United and England, he had never forgotten his younger years in Wythenshawe. Back then, his mum, Melanie, had worked so hard to put food on the table for the family. And if it weren't for the free meals that he got at school, some days Marcus might have gone hungry.

So when the schools closed during the devastating coronavirus pandemic and those free meals stopped, he knew that he had to do something to help. Once upon a time, he had been one of the children who relied on that food and without it, Marcus might not have gone on to achieve his football dreams. He couldn't just sit back and let those kids go hungry; this was his chance to make a difference, to be a gamechanger off the football pitch, as well as on it.

Teaming up with a charity called FareShare, Marcus helped raise almost £1 million. Wow, that was enough money to provide more than 3 million meals per week to vulnerable children across the country!

'Thank you all SO much for the support,' he tweeted. 'And whilst I'm celebrating this, there is SO much more to do.'

As the summer holidays approached, Marcus stood up and spoke out again, sending a public letter to all the MPs in Parliament.

'Please reconsider your decision to cancel the food voucher scheme,' he wrote with passion and understanding. 'This is England in 2020, and this is an issue that needs urgent assistance.'

Marcus' amazing message spread far and wide

through social media, calling on the Prime Minister, Boris Johnson, to act. And it worked! Just one day after his letter, the government announced a new summer food fund for vulnerable children, worth over £120 million.

Although Marcus was the hero of the hour, he was too humble to take the credit.

'Just look at what we can do when we come together,' he told his fans. 'THIS is England in 2020.'

Manchester United

🏆 FA Cup: 2015–16

🏆 League Cup: 2016–17

🏆 UEFA Europa League: 2016–17

🏆 Community Shield: 2017

Individual

🏆 Manchester United Young Player of the Year: 2015–16

🏆 Premier League Player of the Month: January 2019

🏆 Footballer of the Year: 2020

RASHFORD

10 THE FACTS

NAME: Marcus Rashford

DATE OF BIRTH: 31 October 1997

AGE: 23

PLACE OF BIRTH: Wythenshawe, Manchester

NATIONALITY: England

BEST FRIEND: Jesse Lingard

CURRENT CLUB: Manchester United

POSITION: LW

THE STATS

Height (cm):	**185**
Club appearances:	**272**
Club goals:	**90**
Club trophies:	**4**
International appearances:	**39**
International goals:	**11**
International trophies:	**0**
Ballon d'Ors:	**0**

★ ★ ★ **HERO RATING: 86** ★ ★ ★

GREATEST MOMENTS

25 FEBRUARY 2016, MANCHESTER UNITED 5–1 FC MIDTJYLLAND

Due to a late injury to Anthony Martial, Marcus was thrown straight into the United starting line-up for this Europa League second leg match. And at the age of eighteen, he took his chance amazingly well. Marcus played the full ninety minutes, scoring two goals and causing all kinds of problems with his speed and movement. A new star was born at Old Trafford.

20 MARCH 2016, MANCHESTER CITY 0–1 MANCHESTER UNITED

Marcus's incredible first month of first-team football continued with this big Manchester derby. City were the team to beat and United did just that, thanks to a great goal from their new young superstar. Marcus used his speed and skill to beat Martín Demichelis and then calmly shoot past Joe Hart. After only eight games, he was already a United hero.

3 JULY 2018, COLOMBIA 1–1 ENGLAND (WON ON PENALTIES!)

Although Marcus only came on for the last seven minutes of this World Cup Round of 16 match, he still played his part. Manager Gareth Southgate needed his coolest, calmest heads for the penalty shoot-out, and Marcus was certainly one of those. With the pressure on, he went second for England, striking the ball confidently into the bottom corner. Ice-cold!

6 MARCH 2019,
PSG 1–3 MANCHESTER UNITED

Kylian who? Marcus went head-to-head with Mbappé in the Champions League Round of 16 and came out on the winning side. He gave PSG defender Thilo Kehrer a game to forget, setting one goal up for Romelu Lukaku and then scoring the winner from the penalty spot in the last nail-biting seconds. Once again, Marcus had shown that he was a big game player.

30 OCTOBER 2019,
CHELSEA 1–2 MANCHESTER UNITED

On the night before his twenty-second birthday, Marcus proved himself to be United's new star striker. After giving his team the lead with a first-half penalty, he then won the game with a beautiful, swerving free kick from thirty-five yards out. And from that day onwards, Marcus just couldn't stop scoring, reaching nineteen goals by January.

PLAY LIKE YOUR HEROES

THE MARCUS RASHFORD PENALTY ROUTINE

STEP 1: Use your super-speed to race into the opposition box, whether it's you on the ball or one of your teammates. You never know what might happen next…

STEP 2: …PENALTY! As soon as the referee points to the spot, grab the ball and tuck it under your arm. It's yours; don't let anyone take it away from you.

STEP 3: Place it down carefully on the spot, taking a quick look up at the target. Yep, it's still there!

STEP 4: When the referee blows his whistle, take four little shuffles across to the left (that's if you're right-footed, by the way).

STEP 5: Then run forward towards the ball, taking short, stuttering steps to try to fool the keeper.

STEP 6: BANG! Make sure you strike the ball with lots of power, and lots of accuracy too. Aiming for a bottom corner is always best.

STEP 7: GOAL! Keep your celebrations classy and cool, unless, of course, you've just scored a last-minute winner in the Champions League.

TEST YOUR KNOWLEDGE

QUESTIONS

1. Who scored a hat-trick when Marcus went to watch his first-ever Manchester United match?

2. Name at least two other United players who started out at Fletcher Moss Rangers.

3. What did Marcus's brother, Dwaine, do when he first signed for United, aged nine?

4. Marcus used to sneak into the gym to watch which United player practising?

5. Which older United academy players invited Marcus to improve his skills in 'The Cage'?

6. Which Manchester United manager gave Marcus his first team debut?

7. What club trophy did Marcus win at the end of his sensational first season?

8. Marcus played for the England senior team before he played for the Under-21s – true or false?

9. Which three shirt numbers has Marcus worn for Manchester United?

10. Which Manchester United manager helped Marcus to become a better finisher?

11. Which country did Marcus score twice against in the 2018–19 UEFA Nations League?

Answers below. . . No cheating!

1. *The Brazilian Ronaldo (for Real Madrid)* 2. *Any of Wes Brown, Jesse Lingard, Danny Welbeck and Ravel Morrison* 3. *He passed his driving test and bought a car so that he could drive Marcus to training!* 4. *Cristiano Ronaldo* 5. *Paul Pogba, Jesse Lingard and Ravel Morrison* 6. *Louis van Gaal* 7. *The FA Cup* 8. *True! In the one match he played for the Under-21s after Euro 2016, he scored a hat-trick!* 9. *39, 19 and 10* 10. *Ole Gunnar Solskjær* 11. *Spain*

KANE

TABLE OF CONTENTS

CHAPTER 1

ENGLAND HERO

Thursday, 5 October 2017

In the Wembley tunnel, Harry closed his eyes and
soaked up the amazing atmosphere. He was back
at the home of football, the stadium where he had
first achieved his childhood dream of playing for
England. 19 March 2015, England vs Lithuania –
he remembered that game like it was yesterday. He
had scored that day and now, with England facing
Slovenia, he needed to do it again. As England's
captain and Number 9, it was his job to shoot them to
the 2018 World Cup.

'Come on, lads!' Harry called out to his teammates
behind him: friends like Joe Hart, Kyle Walker and

Eric Dier. It was a real honour to be their leader. With a victory over Slovenia, they would all be on their way to the biggest tournament of their lives in Russia.

Harry looked down at the young mascot by his side and smiled at him. 'Right, let's do this!'

As the two of them led the England team out onto the pitch, the fans clapped and cheered. Harry didn't look up at the thousands of faces and flags; instead, he looked down at the grass in front of him. He was totally focused on his task: scoring goals and beating Slovenia.

'If you get a chance, test the keeper,' Harry said to his partners in attack, Raheem Sterling and Marcus Rashford, before kick-off. 'I'll be there for the rebound!'

Harry's new Premiership season with Tottenham Hotspur had not begun well in August, but by September he was back to his lethal best. That month alone, he scored an incredible thirteen goals, including two goals for England against Malta. He could score every type of goal – tap-ins, headers, one-on-ones, long-range shots, penalties, even free kicks. That's what made him such a dangerous striker.

With Slovenia defending well, Harry didn't get many chances in the first half. He got in good positions but the final ball never arrived.

'There's no need to panic yet,' Harry told his teammates in the dressing room. He really didn't want a repeat of England's terrible performance against Iceland at Euro 2016. That match still haunted him. 'We're good enough to win this by playing our natural game. Be patient!'

As Ryan Bertrand dribbled down the left wing, Harry sprinted towards the six-yard box. Ryan's cross didn't reach him but the ball fell to Raheem instead. His shot was going in until a defender deflected it wide.

'Unlucky!' Harry shouted, putting his hands on his head. 'Keep going, we're going to score!'

Without this kind of strong self-belief, Harry would never have made it to the top of European football. There had been lots of setbacks along the way: rejections, disappointments and bad form. But every time, Harry bounced back with crucial goals at crucial moments. That's what made him such a superstar.

A matter of seconds later, a rebound fell to him on the edge of the penalty area. Surely, this was his moment. He pulled back his left foot and curled a powerful shot towards the bottom corner. The fans were already up on their feet, ready to celebrate. Harry never missed… but this time he did. The ball flew just wide of the post. Harry couldn't believe it. He looked up at the sky and sighed.

On the sideline, England manager Gareth Southgate cheered his team on. 'That's much better – the goal is coming, lads!'

But after ninety minutes, the goal still hadn't come. The fourth official raised his board: eight minutes of injury time.

'It's not over yet, boys!' Harry shouted, to inspire his teammates.

The Slovenian goalkeeper tried to throw the ball out to his left-back but Kyle got there first. Straight away, Harry was on the move from the back post to the front post. After playing together for years at Tottenham, they knew how to score great goals.

As Kyle crossed it in, Harry used his burst of speed to get in front of the centre-back. Again, the England supporters stood and waited anxiously. The ball was perfect and Harry stretched out his long right leg to meet it. The keeper got a touch on his shot but he couldn't keep it out.

Goooooooooooooaaaaaaaaaaaaaaaaaaallllllllllllllllllllllll llllll!!!!!!!!!!!!!!!!!!!!!!!!

He had done it! Joy, relief, pride – Harry felt every emotion as he ran towards the fans. This time, he hadn't let them down. He held up the Three Lions on his shirt and screamed until his throat got sore.

'Captain to the rescue!' Kyle laughed as they hugged by the corner flag.

'No, it was all thanks to you!' Harry replied.

At the final whistle, he threw his arms up in the air. It was a phenomenal feeling to qualify for the 2018 World Cup. He couldn't wait to lead England to glory.

'We are off to Russia!' a voice shouted over the loudspeakers and the whole stadium cheered.

It was yet another moment that Harry would

never forget. Against the odds, he was making his childhood dreams come true. He was the star striker for Tottenham, the club that he had supported all his life. And now, like his hero David Beckham, he was the captain of England.

Harry had never given up, even when it looked like he wouldn't make it as a professional footballer. With the support of his family and his coaches, and lots of hard work and dedication, he had proved everyone wrong to become a world-class goal machine.

It had been an incredible journey from Walthamstow to Wembley, and Harry was only just getting started.

CHAPTER 2

ALWAYS KICKING

'Mum!' Charlie shouted, stamping his feet.

Kim sighed and put her magazine down. 'What's happened now?'

'I spent ages building a Lego tower and Harry just kicked it over,' her older son answered. 'That was *my* tower!'

'I'm sorry, darling, but I'm sure Harry didn't mean it. Your brother doesn't know what he's doing with his little feet yet.'

Harry was nearly two years old and he was always on the move around their house in Walthamstow, North London. He had a few bumps on his head but it was his legs that caused the most trouble. Everywhere he went, they never stopped kicking. Kim wasn't surprised, though.

'Do you remember before your brother was born when he was still in my tummy?' she asked Charlie as she lifted Harry up onto the sofa. Charlie didn't reply; he was busy building a new tower. 'He was always kicking, even back then, wasn't he? I didn't get a good night's sleep for months!'

Kim held Harry up in the air to give his legs room to swing. 'No, you don't like letting me sleep, do you?' He smiled and wiggled his hands and feet. 'I knew you'd be a boy; there was no doubt about that. I told your Daddy that you were going to be sporty and do you know what he said? He said, "Great, he'll play for TOTTENHAM!"'

Harry's smile grew wider when he heard the name of their local football club. It was a word that his dad, Pat, said so often that it had become his favourite word. The Kane family lived only five miles away from Tottenham's stadium, White Hart Lane.

'Wow, you really love that idea, don't you!' Kim laughed. 'Well, your Grandad Eric was a good footballer in his day. Maybe you'll get his talent, rather than your Dad's. Bless him, he always says that bad injuries ruined his career but I think it was his bad first touch!'

It was a bright, sunny afternoon and so Kim took her two sons out to the local park. Hopefully, after a few hours of open space and fresh air, Charlie and Harry would sleep well that night, and so would their mum. Once they found a shady spot on the grass, Kim lay down the picnic rug and lifted Harry out of the pushchair.

'Charlie, you've got to stay where I can see you!' she called out as he chased after a squirrel.

After doing a few laps of the rug, Harry sat down and looked around him. He saw leaves and twigs and insects. He saw huge trees above him and patches of blue sky in between. Then his eyes fixed on the exciting scene in front of him. A group of kids were playing football with jumpers for goalposts. That looked like fun. He stood up and went over to explore.

'Harry, stop!' Kim shouted. She chased after her son and scooped him up just before he reached the other kids' football game. In her arms, Harry kept watching and his legs kept moving. He was desperate to kick the ball.

'Not today, darling,' his mum said, giving him a kiss on the cheek. 'But soon, I promise!'

*

'So, how was your day?' Pat asked, as they all ate dinner together. After a long day's work at the garage, he loved to come home to his happy family.

Charlie could now feed himself like a grown-up but Harry still needed a high chair and some help. Even with Pat holding the spoon, Harry got strawberry yoghurt all over his hands and face.

'I built an awesome tower but Harry broke it with his silly little feet,' Charlie told his dad. He was looking for sympathy, but Pat had other ideas.

'Good, your brother's getting ready for his big Tottenham career! Football runs in the family, you know. Just ask your Grandad – I was one of Ireland's best young players but sadly...'

Kim rolled her eyes. Not again! She decided not to mention Harry's kicking in the park. It would only get her husband's hopes up even more.

CHAPTER 3

HEROES AT WHITE HART LANE

'Have you been good boys today?' Pat asked his sons one evening as they all ate dinner together.

Charlie and Harry knew the right answer. 'Yes!'

Their dad smiled and reached into his trouser pocket. He took out three rectangles of white card and placed them down on the table. Then he watched and waited for his sons' reactions.

Harry thought he knew what they were but he didn't want to get his hopes up until he was sure. His dad had promised him that he could go to his first Tottenham game once he turned four. For his birthday, he got a Spurs shirt and a Spurs football, but no Spurs ticket. Charlie had been to White Hart Lane a few times and Harry was desperate to join them. Was his dream finally going to come true? There in the top left corner was the important word, written in navy blue – 'Tottenham'. He was right; they *were* match tickets! Harry jumped for joy.

'Wow, thanks!' he said, running over to give his dad a big hug. 'This is the best gift ever!'

Suddenly, Harry and Charlie weren't interested in eating anymore. Instead, they ran around the living room, waving the tickets in the air and chanting, 'We're going to White Hart Lane! We're going to White Hart Lane!'

Kim laughed. 'You'll need to keep a close eye on them,' she warned her husband. 'This is just the start!'

'Yes, I think I'll look after these,' Pat said, taking the tickets back from his over-excited sons.

It was a three o'clock kick-off on Saturday but Harry and Charlie were sitting in their Tottenham shirts at breakfast. They spent the morning playing football in the garden, pretending to be their heroes.

'David Ginola gets the ball on the left,' Charlie began the commentary, 'he dribbles past one defender and then another. Look at that skill! He's just outside the penalty area now, he looks up and…'

Harry didn't like playing in goal against his brother. He hardly ever made a save because Charlie's shots were too powerful.

…Gooooooooooooooooooaaaaaaaaaallllllllllllllllllllll llllllllllll!!!!!!!!!!!!!!!!!!!!

Charlie ran towards the corner of the garden and celebrated by pulling his Spurs shirt over his head.

'Right, my turn!' Harry said, picking up the ball.

His number one hero, Teddy Sheringham, had just left Tottenham to sign for Manchester United. But Harry already had his new favourite – German Jürgen Klinsmann. It was a hard name for a four-year-old to say but Harry did his best.

'Kiman runs towards the penalty area…'

He needed to strike the ball perfectly if he wanted to score past his older brother. Harry looked up at the goal and kicked it as hard as he could. The ball bounced and skipped towards the bottom corner…

…Gooooooooooooooooooaaaaaaaaaaaaaallllllllllllllll llllllllllll!!!!!!!!!!!!!!!!!!!!

Normally, Harry celebrated with the Klinsmann dive

but his Spurs shirt was white and he couldn't make his White Hart Lane debut wearing a muddy shirt! So instead, he jumped up and pumped his fist. He could tell that it was going to be a very good day.

After lunch, it was finally time for them to leave.

'Have you got your hats?' Kim asked at the front door.

Harry nodded.

'Gloves?'

Harry nodded.

'Good, stay close to your dad and have a great time!'

They were off! Harry couldn't wait to get to White Hart Lane. On the bus, he imagined the people, the noise, the goals. As they crossed through the Walthamstow reservoirs, Charlie had a thought.

'Dad, have you got the tickets?'

There was panic on Pat's face as he checked all of his pockets, once and then twice. 'Oh dear,' he muttered.

Harry's face dropped with disappointment. How

had his dad forgotten the tickets? Why hadn't he checked before they left?

Suddenly, a smile spread across Pat's face, and he held up the tickets. 'Just kidding!' he cheered.

'Dad, don't scare us like that!' Harry shouted. He didn't find the joke funny at all.

When they got off the bus, the stadium was right there in front of them. Harry stood there looking up, his mouth wide open. It was even bigger than he'd expected.

'Come on, let's go in and find our seats!' his dad said. 'Don't let go of my hand, okay? If you get lost, Mum won't ever let us come back.'

Harry held on tightly as they moved through the crowds towards the turnstile, on their way to their seats. There were so many people everywhere and so much to see and hear.

'Get today's match programme here!' the sellers shouted.

Some Tottenham fans talked about their players in between bites of burgers and hot dogs. Other Tottenham fans were already singing songs even before they entered the stadium. It was all so exciting.

Once they were through the turnstile, Harry could see a square of green in the distance. His eyes lit up – the pitch! As they got closer, he couldn't believe the size of it. How did the players keep running from box to box for ninety minutes? It looked impossible.

'Look, there's Ginola!' Charlie shouted, pointing down at the players warming up. 'And there's Klinsmann!'

Harry stood up on his seat to get a better view. He was in the same stadium as his heroes; it didn't get any better than that.

Tottenham, Tottenham!

As the players ran out of the tunnel for the start of the game, the noise grew even louder. Spurs needed a win to stay out of the relegation zone. After a few minutes, Ginola got the ball on the left wing.

'Come on!' the Tottenham fans cheered, rising to their feet.

Ginola curled a brilliant cross into the penalty area. Harry held his breath as Klinsmann stretched to reach it...

Goooooooooooooooooooooaaaaaaaaaaaaaaaaaalllllll llllllllllllllllllll!!!!!!!!!!!!!!!!!!!!

What a start! Harry and Charlie jumped up and down together, cheering for their heroes.

The rest of the match was very tense but Tottenham held on for the victory. By the final whistle, Harry was exhausted but very happy. He was already looking forward to his next trip to White Hart Lane.

'So, who was man of the match?' Pat asked his sons on the bus home.

'Ginola!' Charlie replied.

'Klinsmann!' Harry replied.

Their dad shook his head. 'If we ever keep a clean sheet, it's always the goalkeeper!'

CHAPTER 4

RIDGEWAY ROVERS

'Why do we have to leave?' Charlie cried out. 'It's not fair. This is our home!'

Their parents had just given them some terrible news; the family was moving from Walthamstow to Chingford. They had never even heard of Chingford.

'We'll have more space there,' Kim replied. 'You'll have bigger bedrooms and a bigger football pitch in the garden too.'

'Look, we're not talking about Australia!' Pat said. 'Chingford is only a few miles away.'

'But all our friends are *here*,' Charlie argued.

As the conversation carried on, Harry had an important question to ask: 'How far is it from White Hart Lane?'

'It's only five miles away, the same distance as now.'

Kim and Pat finally won the family argument with a killer fact: David Beckham had grown up in Chingford.

'Really?' Harry asked excitedly. After the 1998 World Cup, Beckham was England's most famous footballer. Despite his red card versus Argentina, every kid in the country wanted to look and play like Becks.

His dad nodded. 'He played for a local team called Ridgeway Rovers.'

'Cool, can I play for Ridgeway Rovers too?'

'It's a deal!' Kim said, looking relieved.

Harry was determined to become a star striker for Tottenham and England, especially after visiting White Hart Lane. He practised all the time, with whatever he could find. In the garden and the park, he played with his own real football. It was his pride and joy, and he looked after it carefully. In the street, he played with any can or bottle that he could find. In the house, he swapped his football for rolled-up socks.

'STOP KICKING THINGS!' Charlie shouted angrily

from through his bedroom door.

'Sorry!' Harry replied quickly, running downstairs to help with dinner. He had been using his brother's door as a shooting target again. He knew that it wasn't allowed but he just couldn't help himself.

'Can I join Ridgeway Rovers now?' Harry asked his parents as they sat down to eat. He was desperate to test his talent against real opponents on a real pitch.

Pat knew that his son wasn't going to give up until it was sorted. Fifteen minutes later, he returned to the living room with good news. 'The Ridgeway Rovers trials are coming up in a couple of weeks. I'll take you along.'

'Thanks!' Harry cheered. He couldn't wait to follow in Becks' footsteps. But first, he had lots more practice to do.

'It's great to see so many of you down here,' Dave Bricknell, the Ridgeway Rovers coach, told the eager young faces at Loughton Rugby Club. 'Welcome! Today, we're looking for brilliant new players to join our club, but most importantly, we're going to have some fun, yes?'

'YES!' Harry cheered with the other boys.

As they all practised passing in pairs, Dave walked around the pitch. He was looking for a nice touch, as well as accuracy and power in the pass.

'Very good!' he called out to Harry.

Next up was dribbling. It wasn't Harry's favourite skill but he managed to keep the ball under control as he weaved in and out of the cones. He was relieved when it was over and he had only knocked one over.

'Right, it's the moment you've all been waiting for,' Dave said to the group. 'Shooting! Do we have a goalkeeper here?'

Everyone looked around but no-one stepped forward.

The coach looked surprised. 'Really? Not a single keeper?'

Harry was really looking forward to scoring some goals but he also didn't mind playing in goal, especially if it wasn't Charlie who was shooting at him. Slowly, he raised his arm.

'Great! What's your name?' Dave asked.

'Harry.'

'Thanks, Harry! You'll get a chance to shoot later on, I promise.'

He put on a pair of gloves, walked over to the goal and waited. As the first shot came towards him, he didn't even have to move. He caught the ball and rolled it to the side. The next shot was better and he had to throw himself across the goal to tip it round the post.

'What a save, Harry!' Dave clapped. 'I think we've found our new keeper!'

Harry enjoyed diving around but he didn't want to be Ian Walker or David Seaman. He wanted to be Teddy Sheringham or Jürgen Klinsmann.

'Coach,' he called out after the first round of shots, 'I don't really play in goal. I normally play outfield as a striker.'

'Not again!' Dave thought to himself. Young keepers always got bored and asked to move to attack for the glory. Even so, he made a promise to the boy:

'No problem, I'll put you up front for the match at the end. You're a natural in goal, though!'

Harry waited patiently for his chance to shine. It

took a little while, even once the match had started. But finally, his teammate kicked a long pass down the pitch and he was off, sprinting as fast as his little legs could go. He wasn't the fastest but he had a head start because of his clever run.

Harry beat the defender to the ball, took one touch to control it and calmly placed his shot in the bottom corner.

Gooooooooooooooooooaaaaaaaaaaaaaaaalllllllllllllll llllllllllllll!!!!!!!!!!!!!!!!!!!!

Ten minutes later, Harry had a hat-trick and a place in the Ridgeway Rovers team.

'You're a natural keeper *and* a natural striker,' Dave laughed. 'I guess you're just a natural footballer!'

Harry couldn't wait for the real matches to begin. As he stepped out onto the field for the first time in the blue and white Ridgeway Rovers shirt, he felt unstoppable. This was it. He was ready for the big time, but was the big time ready for him?

When the ball came to him in the penalty area, Harry took a shot and it deflected off a defender and out for a corner.

'I'll take it!' Harry shouted, chasing over to the flag.

It was a long way from the corner to the penalty area, so he kicked it as hard as he could. The ball flew over the heads of everyone, including the goalkeeper. It landed in the back of the net.

Goooooooooooooaaaaaaaaaaaaaaaallllllllllllllllllllllll llllll!!!!!!!!!!!!!!!!!!!!!

Harry punched the air with joy – he was off the mark on his debut! It was a lucky strike but that didn't matter. Would he ever get tired of scoring goals? He really didn't think so.

CHAPTER 5

FOOTBALL, FOOTBALL, FOOTBALL

'That's it! Keep your head steady and lean over the ball as you kick it.'

At the weekends, Harry's dad often helped him with extra training in the back garden. There was so much that he wanted to improve, especially his shooting. He couldn't relax if he wanted to keep his place as Ridgeway Rovers' number one striker.

'Right, I think that's enough,' Pat said after an hour. 'You've got a game later today and you'll be too tired to score.'

'Okay, just three more shots,' Harry begged.

If his dad was busy, he went to the park with Charlie. When Harry was younger, his older brother used to make him stand between two trees and try to save his powerful shots for hours. That wasn't much fun but now that he was eight, Charlie let him join in properly. If there were other kids around, they'd play a big match but if it was just the two of them, they had long, competitive one-on-one battles. Harry was a skilful footballer but his older brother had one weapon that could defeat him: strength.

'Come on, that's not fair!' Harry shouted as he picked himself up off the grass. 'You can't just push me off the ball like that.'

Charlie shrugged. 'That was a shoulder-to-shoulder challenge. It's not my fault that I'm bigger than you.'

It was no use complaining; Harry just had to find other ways to beat his brother. Luckily, he was very determined. A few times he stormed off angrily but most of the time, Harry tried and tried until he succeeded.

'You're definitely getting better, bro!' Charlie told him as they walked back home together for lunch.

Harry smiled proudly; that was his aim. He didn't want to just be an average player; he wanted to become a great player like his Tottenham heroes. He didn't care how much time and effort that would take. Harry played football before school, at break-time, at lunchtime, and then after school too.

'See you later, Mum!' he called out as he gulped down a glass of water and threw his bag down.

Kim didn't need to ask where her son was going. She knew exactly where he would be and what he'd be doing. 'Just be careful and make sure you're back for dinner,' was all she said.

In the summer, Harry and his friends played in the park all day. But in the winter, it was too dark so they swapped grass for tarmac. Under the streetlights, their games could go on much longer, although there were more obstacles to deal with.

'Stop!' Harry called out. 'Car coming!'

All shots had to be low and soft. A few broken flowers were fine but broken windows meant game over.

'Kev, don't blast it!'

'Mrs Curtis is watching at the curtain!'

Harry loved their street games because they really

helped him to improve his technique. In the tight space between the pavements, his control had to be excellent and he had to look up quickly to find the pass. His movement had to be good too if he wanted to escape from the defenders and score.

'Yes!' he would scream as he made a sudden run towards goal. If he got it right, his marker wouldn't have time to turn and catch him.

Harry's hero, Teddy Sheringham, was back as Tottenham's Number 10. He watched him carefully in every match and tried to copy his movement. Teddy wasn't the quickest striker in the Premier League but he was always alert and clever around the penalty area.

'Stay tight on Harry,' his opponents would say. 'Don't switch off or he'll score!'

Normally, their street games were friendly and fun, but not always. If the result came down to next goal wins, everyone took it very seriously.

'No way! That went straight over the jumper – that's not a goal.'

'What are you talking about? That was post and in!'

'Stop cheating!'

'You're the one who's cheating!'

Of course, there was no referee, so Harry often had to be the peacemaker. He wanted to win just as much as the other boys, if not more, but he always stayed calm. Getting angry didn't help anyone. If Harry ended up on the losing team one day, he just worked even harder the next day.

Harry's days started and ended with football. It was all he thought about. In bed, he lay there imagining his Tottenham debut:

It was 0–0 with ten minutes to go and he came on to replace Les Ferdinand up front. Darren Anderton got the ball in midfield and played a brilliant through-ball. Harry ran towards goal, and he was one-on-one with the goalkeeper. Could he stay calm and find the net?

Unfortunately, he fell asleep before he found out the answer.

CHAPTER 6

ARSENAL

Harry was used to seeing Premier League scouts at Ridgeway Rovers matches. There was lots of young talent in north east London and no club wanted to miss out on the next David Beckham. If he kept scoring, Harry believed that it could be him.

'Well played, today,' said Ian Marshall, the Chairman of Ridgeway Rovers, as he ruffled the boy's short hair. 'How many is that for the season now?'

Harry pretended to count but he knew the answer. 'Eighteen in fifteen games.'

'You're our little Alan Shearer!'

Harry shook his head. 'I prefer Sheringham.'

Ian laughed. 'Of course, Teddy it is then! Do you mind if I have a quick chat with your dad please?'

While Harry practised his keepie-uppies nearby, the adults chatted.

'We had an Arsenal scout here today,' Ian said. 'He wants your boy to go for a trial there.'

Pat wasn't surprised; he already knew that his son was a very good player. But he wanted to do what was best for him.

'What do you think?' he asked Ian. 'He's still only eight – is he too young to join an academy? I want Harry to keep enjoying his football.'

The Ridgeway Rovers coach nodded. 'I understand. Look, I don't think there's any harm in him trying it out. If he doesn't like it, he can just come back here. We'll always have a place for him.'

Pat thanked Ian. 'Harry loves everything about football but I just don't want to get his hopes up. It can be a very cruel business for youngsters.'

As soon as they were in the car, Harry wanted to know everything. 'What were you and Ian talking about?'

'Wait until we get home. I need to talk to your mum first.'

'Okay, but was it a Tottenham scout?'

'Harry!'

'A West Ham scout?'

'HARRY!'

After a whispered chat with Kim in the kitchen, Pat shared the good news with his son. 'Arsenal want to offer you a trial. What do you think?'

Harry's first thoughts were a mix of pride and disappointment. It was amazing news that a Premier League club wanted him, but why did it have to be Arsenal, Tottenham's biggest rivals?

'But we hate Arsenal, Dad!'

Pat laughed. 'We don't really hate them, son. It's just a football rivalry. They're a great club and they're doing very well at the moment.'

His dad was right; Arsenal were the second-best team in England, just behind Manchester United. They had exciting superstars like Dennis Bergkamp, Patrick Vieira and Thierry Henry. Tottenham, meanwhile, were down in mid-table.

That was enough to make Harry change his mind. 'Okay, so when can I start?'

For the big day, Harry decided not to wear his Tottenham shirt. He was already going to be the new kid at Arsenal and he didn't want to make things even harder.

'How are you feeling?' his mum asked on the journey to London Colney, Arsenal's training ground location.

'Fine,' Harry replied but really, he was getting more and more nervous in the backseat of the car. It was going to be a massive challenge for him, and what if he failed? What if he wasn't good enough and made a fool of himself? This wasn't Ridgeway Rovers anymore.

'You'll be brilliant,' Kim told him, giving his hand a squeeze. 'But maybe don't tell your new coaches that you're a Spurs fan straight away!'

Harry smiled and felt a bit more relaxed. As long as he tried his best, what more could he do?

As they drove into the Arsenal Training Centre, Harry couldn't believe his eyes. Compared to Ridgeway's Peter May Sports Centre, it looked like a whole city. There were ten perfect, full-size pitches, as well as lots of indoor facilities.

'Not bad, is it?' his dad joked.

Once the session began, Harry's nerves turned into adrenaline. 'I can do this!' he told himself. Everything felt better with a football at his feet.

In the drills, he showed off his best touch and passing. Some of the other boys had incredible technique already, but Harry didn't let that get him down. He was waiting for his moment to shine – shooting. When that moment arrived, the Arsenal goalkeepers didn't have a chance. Bottom left, top right, straight down the middle; Harry scored every time.

'Great work!' the coach clapped.

That trial session soon turned into a whole season at Arsenal. At first, it felt strange to play for Tottenham's enemies but Harry soon forgot about that. He was having so much fun. He wasn't as skilful as some of his teammates, but that wasn't really his role – he was the one who scored the goals. He didn't play every minute of every match but he tried to make the most of every opportunity.

At the end of the season, the Arsenal academy had to choose which youngsters to keep and which youngsters to let go. Harry crossed his fingers tightly for weeks but unfortunately, it was bad news. The coaches decided that he was too small for his age.

'I'm so sorry,' his dad said, giving him a hug. 'Be proud and keep going. Once you've had your growth spurt, Arsenal are going to regret it!'

For the next few days, Harry was so angry and upset that he wanted to give up. But luckily, that feeling didn't last long. He realised that he loved football too much to stop. If Arsenal didn't want him, he knew another team that hopefully still did.

'Dad, can I go and play for Ridgeway Rovers again?'

The Peter May Sports Centre would always feel like home.

'Welcome back, kid!' Ian said with a wink. 'What we're looking for is a goalscorer, a fox in the box – do you know of anyone like that?'

Harry grinned. 'Yes – me!'

CHAPTER 7

CHINGFORD FOUNDATION SCHOOL

After playing for Ridgeway Rovers, Harry was soon following in David Beckham's footsteps for a second time when he started at Chingford Foundation School. Becks' signed shirt hung proudly in the entrance lobby at Chingford. Harry looked at it every morning as he arrived at school, hoping that it would bring him luck, but especially on the day of the trial for the Year 7 football team. Chingford had one of the best track records in Greater London and Harry was ready to be their next star.

'I'm the striker that they need and I'll show them at the trial,' he told his brother, Charlie, on the way to school. He wasn't quite as confident as he sounded but he was as determined as ever.

Harry loved scoring goals. It was an amazing feeling when a shot hit the back of the net. But he could do a lot more than just that. During his year at Arsenal, he had improved his all-round game. He was good in possession, and creative too. Setting up chances for his teammates was almost as much fun as scoring.

'Just don't be too selfish,' Charlie warned. 'Mr Leadon hates a show-off!'

Harry didn't forget his brother's advice. After changing into his white Tottenham shirt, he made his way out onto the pitch with the other boys.

'Good luck!' Harry told his mates. They were all competing for places now.

After a warm-up and some passing exercises, Mark Leadon, Chingford's football coach, split the boys up and gave half of them orange bibs.

'I'm looking for team players today,' he told them. 'If you just want to show off how many tricks you can do, go do that in the playground. I want to see how you can work together and help each other to win.

Right, let's play!'

Most of Harry's schoolmates knew that he was a good footballer because they had seen him play in the lunchtime games. They knew that he had played for Arsenal, but he was still quite small and he didn't have the flashy skills and speed to dribble past everyone. There were other boys who looked more talented but Harry hadn't played at his best. Yet.

'If we pass the ball around, they'll get tired and the chances will come,' he told his teammates. He had made himself the leader.

Harry was ready to be patient but he didn't need to be. The opposition defenders couldn't cope with his clever runs into space. As the cross came in, he made a late run to beat his marker to the ball.

Goooooooooooooooooaaaaaaaaaaaaaaaaaaaallllllllllllllllll llllllllllllll!!!!!!!!!!!!!!!!!!!!!!

Harry didn't run off and celebrate on his own; he ran straight to thank the teammate who had set him up. Together, they ran back for the restart. They had more goals to score.

'I like this kid,' Mark thought to himself on

the sidelines. 'For an eleven-year-old, he really understands football. He knows where to go and he knows where his teammates are going to go too.'

Harry didn't stop running until Mark blew the whistle to end the game. By then, it had turned into a thrashing. When he found room to shoot, Harry shot and scored. When he could see another player in space, he passed for them to score instead. He was involved in every part of his team's victory.

They walked off the pitch together, with their arms around each other's shoulders. Their man of the match was right at the centre of the gang.

'Well played,' Mark said to them but he was looking straight at Harry.

'Thanks, sir,' he replied politely, but inside, he was buzzing with pride.

Mark was very impressed. Every year, he had excellent young footballers in his school team but this boy seemed special. He had technique, vision, movement *and* work-rate. Mark could tell that it was going to be a good season.

'So, how did it go?' Charlie asked when his brother

got home from school that evening.

Harry smiled and shrugged modestly. 'It went okay, I think.'

Harry became the first name on a very successful teamsheet. His goals led Chingford to school cup glory.

'If you keep working hard, your shirt could be hanging up there with Becks one day!' Mark Leadon told him.

CHAPTER 8

HEROES AND DREAMS

'Welcome!' David Beckham announced to a group of sixteen boys and girls. The England superstar was in East London to launch his brand-new football academy. With his white Adidas tracksuit and trendy haircut, he looked so cool. 'Today, we're going to practise some of my favourite skills.'

Harry wasn't really listening; he was too busy staring at his hero. He was one of the Chingford Foundation School footballers who had been selected to go to the academy launch. So now, Becks was right next to him, giving him football tips! Surely, it was too good to be true? But no, it was really happening.

Like Becks, Harry wore an Adidas tracksuit, but

their hairstyles didn't match. Harry's head was shaved short, like Becks way back in 2000, but Becks had tried five different looks since then! Harry felt very nervous. Not only was Becks watching him but there were also cameras everywhere. Still, he was desperate to impress. Harry dribbled the ball carefully from end to end, and kept his keepie-uppies simple.

'That's it, great work everyone!' Becks called out.

At the end of the day, he shook each of them by the hand and chatted with them. When it was Harry's turn, he was too nervous and shy to speak. Luckily, Becks went first.

'Well done today. Are you one of the lads from Chingford?' he asked.

Harry nodded. 'A-and I play for Ridgeway Rovers too.'

Becks smiled. 'Great club, so what's next? What's your dream?'

Harry didn't need to think about that one. 'I want to play for England at Wembley!'

'Good choice, it's the best feeling in the world. If

you keep working hard, you can do it. Good luck!'

As Harry travelled home with his mum, he could still hear his hero's inspirational words in his head – 'you can do it'.

*

'Play the pass now!' Harry shouted, as he sprinted towards goal. It was only one of their street games, but that didn't matter. Every football match was important. The pass never arrived, however.

'Car!' one of his mates shouted, picking up the ball.

As he moved over towards the pavement, Harry noticed two strange things about this particular car. Firstly, it wasn't the typical old banger that usually drove through the area. It was a huge black Range Rover and it looked brand-new. Secondly, the car didn't speed off once they were out of the way. Instead, it stopped and the driver's door opened.

'Hey guys, do you fancy a game?' the man said with a big smile on his face.

Harry's jaw dropped. Was he dreaming? Was Jermain Defoe, Spurs' star striker, really standing there asking to play with them?

'Yes, Jermain's on our team!'

'Hey, that's not fair!'

After a few minutes of arguing, the decision was made: Harry and Jermain would play on opposite teams.

'Let's see what you've got!' Jermain told him with a wink.

Harry loved a challenge but this one was impossible. He knew that he couldn't compete with a top Premier League striker yet but he did his best. He chased every pass and got on the ball as often as possible. He wanted to show off all his skills.

When he wasn't racing around the pitch, Harry tried to watch his superstar opponent in action. Jermain scored lots of goals but Harry was more interested in the rest of his play. With a powerful burst of speed, he could escape from any tackle. Jermain was always thinking one step ahead, playing quick passes to get his teammates into really dangerous areas. If there was a loose ball, or a goalmouth scramble, he was always the first to react.

First Becks and now Jermain; Harry was learning from the very best.

After half an hour, Jermain had to leave. 'Thanks for the game, lads!'

The boys all stood and watched as the black Range Rover drove away. Then they looked at each other, their faces full of wonder. It was a night that none of them would ever forget.

'They're not going to believe us at school, are they?' Harry said.

His mates shook their heads. 'Not in a million years.'

CHAPTER 9

TOTTENHAM AT LAST

'I can't believe you're leaving us again,' Ian Marshall said with a wink and a handshake. 'I hope it goes well for you, lad, but if not, just come back home!'

Harry would miss playing for Ridgeway Rovers but Watford had offered him a trial. They weren't as big as Arsenal or Tottenham, but they were a good Championship team. It was the sort of new challenge that he needed.

'Good luck!' Pat called from the car window as he dropped Harry off at the Watford training centre. His son hadn't said much during the journey and he hoped that he wasn't brooding on his experience at

Arsenal. Harry was at a different club now and there was nothing to worry about.

But Harry wasn't worried; he was just focused on doing his best. He might only have a few weeks to impress his new coaches, so he had to get things right. If Harry missed one shot, he had to score the next one.

'How did it go?' Pat asked when he returned to pick him up.

'It was good,' was all Harry said. This time, he was taking it one step at a time. He didn't want to get carried away. It was just nice to be training with a professional team again.

But it turned out that Watford weren't the only ones chasing him. Another club was also interested, the only club in Harry's heart – Tottenham.

Tottenham's youth scout Mark O'Toole had been watching Harry's Ridgeway Rovers performances for nearly a year. Harry was easily the best player in his team. He was a natural finisher and he had good technique. So, what was Mark waiting for?

'He knows exactly where the goal is but most

strikers are either big or quick,' he discussed with the
other scouts. 'Harry's neither!'

Mark liked to be 100 per cent certain before he told
the Tottenham youth coaches to offer a youngster a
trial. But when he heard that Harry was at Watford,
he decided to take a risk, and advised the coaches:

'I want you to take a look at a kid who plays for
Ridgeway Rovers. He scores lots of goals but he's
not a classic striker. I guess he's more like Teddy
Sheringham than Alan Shearer.'

'Interesting! What's his name?'

'Harry Kane.'

'Well, tell him to come down for a trial.'

When his dad told him the news, Harry thought his
family were playing a prank on him. How could they
be so mean? Surely, they knew how much he wanted
to play for his local club.

'No, I'm serious!' Pat told him. He tried to look
serious but he couldn't stop smiling. 'I got a call from
a Tottenham youth scout. They want you to go down
to the training centre next week.'

After checking a few times, Harry celebrated with a

lap of the living room.

'I'm going to play for Tottenham! I'm going to play for Tottenham!'

He had only been training with Watford for about a month, but there was no way that he could say no to Spurs. His dream team was calling him.

Harry waited and worried but finally the big day arrived.

'How are you feeling?' Pat asked as they drove to Spurs Lodge in Epping Forest.

Harry nodded. His heart was beating so fast that he thought it might jump out of his mouth if he tried to speak.

'Just remember to enjoy it, son,' his dad told him. 'It's a big opportunity but you've got to have fun, okay?'

Harry nodded again. Nothing was as fun as scoring goals.

As they parked their car, Harry could see the other boys warming up on the pitch. In their matching club tracksuits, they seemed to be having a great time together. This was the Under-13s but they all looked at least fifteen. Harry was still waiting for his growth spurt. What if they didn't want a little kid to join their group? What if he made a fool of himself? No, he couldn't think like that. He had to keep believing in himself.

Mark O'Toole was there at the entrance to greet them. 'Welcome to Tottenham! Are you ready for this, kid?'

This time, Harry had to speak. 'Yes, thanks.'

After a deep breath, he walked out onto the pitch in his lucky Tottenham shirt. He had nothing to lose.

Two hours later, Harry was on his way back home, sweaty and buzzing.

'They scored first but I knew we would win it. We had all the best players. George is really good in midfield and Danny can dribble past anyone. I reckon he can kick it even harder than Charlie! The other team didn't stand a chance, really. We had to work hard but–'

'Whoa, slow down, kiddo!' his dad laughed. 'So, you had a good time out there?'

'It was so much fun! I scored the winning goal!'

'I know – it was a great strike too.'

Harry frowned. 'How do you know that?'

His dad laughed. 'I watched from the car! I didn't want to put extra pressure on you by standing there on the sidelines but I wasn't going to miss your first session. Well done, you played really well tonight.'

After six weeks on trial, Harry became a proper Spurs youth team player. It was the proudest moment of his life but he had lots of hard work ahead of him. He had been the best player at Ridgeway Rovers, but he was now just average at Tottenham. It was like starting school all over again.

Luckily, Harry was a quick and willing learner. If it meant he got to play for Spurs, he would do anything the coaches asked him to do.

'Excellent effort, Harry!' John Moncur, the head of youth development, shouted.

Harry was enjoying himself but as summer approached, he began to worry. Soon, it would be time for the end-of-season letters again. Would Spurs decide to keep him for another year? After his experience at Arsenal, he couldn't bear another rejection. The day the post arrived, Harry's hands were shaking.

'Open it!' his brother Charlie demanded impatiently.

When he tore open the envelope, Harry read the dreaded word and his heart sank: '*Unfortunately…*'. It was the release letter. He tried to hold back the tears but he couldn't. 'I don't understand – I had a good season!'

The phone rang and Pat went to answer it. Within seconds, the sadness was gone from his voice. Instead, he sounded relieved. 'Don't worry, these things happen…Yes, I'll tell him right now.'

'Panic over!' Pat called out as he returned to the living room. Harry looked up and saw a big smile on his dad's face. What was going on? 'They sent you the wrong letter by mistake. Spurs want you to stay!'

CHAPTER 10

ONE MORE YEAR

Alex Inglethorpe was Tottenham's Under-18s coach but once a week, he helped out with the Under-14s training. He liked to keep an eye on the younger age groups because the most talented boys would soon move up into his team. Ryan Mason and Andros Townsend were already making the step-up. Who would be next?

During the session, Alex offered lots of advice, especially to the team's best players. There were a couple of speedy full-backs, plus a tall centre-back and a classy playmaker in central midfield. And then there was Harry.

Harry didn't really stand out as an amazing young

footballer, but Alex loved the boy's attitude. He played with so much desire and all he wanted to do was score goals for his team. Harry understood that he wasn't as strong or quick as the other strikers, but he didn't let that stop him. He loved a challenge, and competing with Tottenham's best young players was certainly a challenge. With the pressure on, he never panicked. He just made the most of his technique and worked hard on his weaknesses.

'That's it, Harry! Shield the ball from the defender and wait until the pass is on. Lovely!'

Harry was the perfect student. After most sessions, he would stay behind for extra shooting practice. For a youth coach, that desire was a very good sign.

'Let's wait and see what happens when he grows a bit,' Alex kept telling everyone at the Tottenham academy. But they couldn't wait forever. Next year, Harry would be moving up to the Under-16s. Before then, they had to make a big decision about his future.

'Thanks for coming,' the Under-14s coach said, shaking hands with Harry's parents. 'I wanted to talk to you about your son's progress. As you know, everyone loves Harry here at Spurs. He works so hard and he's a pleasure to work with.'

Pat and Kim could tell that there was a 'But' coming.

'But we're worried. He's still small for his age and he's not a speedy little striker like Jermain Defoe. Don't get me wrong, Harry's got a very good understanding of the game but he needs more than just that if he wants to play up front for Spurs.'

'Okay, so how long does he have to get better?' Pat asked. Once they knew the timeframe, they could make a plan.

The Under-14s coach frowned. 'Every age group is a big new challenge and unless we see real improvement, we don't think that Harry will make it in the Under-16s next year.'

So, one more year. When they got home, Pat sat Harry down in the living room and told him the news. He could see the tears building in his son's eyes. First Arsenal and now Tottenham...

'Don't worry, this isn't over,' Pat said, putting an arm around Harry's shoulder. 'We just have to work even harder to prove them wrong. We believe in you. Do you want to give up?'

Harry shook his head firmly. 'No.'

His dad smiled. 'Good, that's my boy! We'll make a plan tomorrow.'

For the next twelve months, Harry trained with Tottenham as normal, but he also did extra sessions away from the club.

'I want to help but me and you kicking a ball around in the garden won't cut it anymore,' his dad joked. 'It's time to get serious!'

At first, 'serious' just meant lots of boring running and not much actual football. Harry did short sprints until he could barely lift his legs. 'What's the point of this?' he thought to himself as he stood there panting in the rain. This wasn't the beautiful game that he loved.

'Let's have a chat,' his coach said. He could tell that Harry was hating every second of it. 'Look kid, you're never going to be a 100-metre champion but a short burst of pace can make a huge difference for a striker.'

Harry thought back to Jermain Defoe during that street game a few years earlier. He was really good at making space for the shot and his reaction speed was amazing. That was what Harry needed. If the ball dropped in the penalty area, he had to get there first. If a goalkeeper made a save, he had to win the race to the rebound.

'Brilliant, Harry!' his coach cried out a few minutes later. 'That's your best time yet!'

Soon, they moved on to ball work. Harry practised his hold-up play, his heading and, of course, his shooting. He could feel the improvement and so could Tottenham. After a few months, Harry was looking fitter and much more confident on the pitch. Most importantly, he was a better striker and he was scoring more goals.

'Congratulations, kid!' Alex told him after another brilliant performance. 'I knew you'd prove them wrong. And you're getting taller every time I see you.'

Yes, Harry was finally growing! Everything was falling into place at just the right time. Thanks to lots of extra effort, Spurs wanted him to stay. Now, Harry just needed to grow into his tall new body.

CHAPTER 11

MEXICO AND SWITZERLAND

By the time he turned fifteen, Harry had become one of Tottenham's hottest prospects. He still played a lot of games for the Under-16s but he was also getting experience at higher levels. No matter who he played against, Harry kept scoring goals.

'That kid is one of the best natural finishers I've ever seen,' Spurs coach Tim Sherwood told Alex Inglethorpe. 'Why have I never heard of him until now?'

The Under-18s coach laughed. 'He's a late developer!'

'Okay, well look after him carefully – he could be our next goal machine.'

At the start of the 2008–09 season, Jonathan Obika had been Alex's number one striker in the Spurs academy side but the team played lots of matches and it was good to have competition for places.

'Welcome to the squad!' Alex said as he gave Harry the good news. 'At first, you'll be on the bench but if you keep making the most of your opportunities, you'll force your way into the starting line-up. You deserve this.'

Harry was delighted. Not only was he moving up but he was joining a very good side. There was Steven Caulker at the back, Ryan Mason in the middle and Andros Townsend on the wing. With teammates like that, he was going to get plenty of chances to score. Harry couldn't wait.

'If I grab a few goals, I could be playing for the first team soon!' he told Charlie excitedly.

It was his older brother's job to keep his feet on the ground. 'And if you miss a few sitters, you could be playing for the Under-16s again!' Charlie teased.

Luckily, that didn't happen. Harry kept on scoring and soon he was off on an exciting international adventure.

'I'm going to Mexico!' he told his family in December. 'I made the Spurs team for the Copa Chivas.'

'Never heard of it!' Charlie replied with a smile. He was very proud of his younger brother, but it wasn't very cool to show it.

Kim was more concerned about Christmas. 'When do you leave?' she asked.

Harry shrugged; he wasn't bothered about the details. He was playing football for Tottenham; that was all he needed to know. 'In January, I think.'

It was going to be the trip of a lifetime. He couldn't wait to have lots of fun with Ryan, Steven and Andros and win the tournament. What an experience it would be!

'Just you behave yourself,' his mum told him at the airport. 'Don't let the older boys get you into trouble!'

After a long flight, the squad arrived in Guadalajara and found the familiar Tottenham cockerel on the side of a big coach.

'We're famous!' Ryan joked as they all got on board.

In the Copa Chivas, Tottenham faced teams from Spain, Costa Rica, Brazil, Paraguay, Norway and, of course, Mexico.

'Come on boys, we're representing England here!' Harry said, looking down at their white Spurs shirts.

It was hard work in the heat but Tottenham did well. In eight matches, Harry managed to score three goals.

'Only Ryan got more than me!' he told his parents proudly when he returned to Chingford. It had been the best trip ever, but he was glad to get back to his own bedroom and home cooking.

A few months later, Harry was off again. Tottenham were playing in the *Torneo Bellinzona* in Switzerland against big clubs like Sporting Lisbon and Barcelona.

'Barca who?' Steven joked. They weren't scared of anyone.

Harry started two of their five matches and, although he didn't score, he played a big role in helping his team to win the tournament.

'I like setting up goals too, you know!' he reminded Ryan after their final win. It was a great feeling but nothing beat scoring goals.

Harry had really enjoyed his travels and he had learnt a lot from playing against teams from other countries. But back in England, it was time to think about his Spurs future. With his sixteenth birthday coming up, would Tottenham offer him a scholarship contract? He felt like he was improving all the time but he didn't want to get his hopes up. As time went by, his fears grew.

'Harry, have you got any plans for Tuesday?' John McDermott, the head of the academy, asked him casually.

He quickly worked out the date in his head. 'That's my birthday! Why?'

John smiled. 'Do you think you'll have time to come in and sign your contract?

Harry had never felt so relieved. He couldn't wait to tell his family and friends. After all his hard work, he was finally getting his reward. Signing with Spurs would be the best birthday present ever.

CHAPTER 12

GETTING CLOSER

Ahead of the 2009–10 season, the Tottenham Under-18s lined up for their squad photo. Harry had grown so much that the cameraman placed him on the back row next to the goalkeepers. He wasn't yet important enough to sit in the front row, but that was where he aimed to be next year.

Once everyone was in position, the cameraman counted down. '3, 2, 1... Click!'

Most of his teammates looked very serious in the photos but Harry couldn't help smiling. Why shouldn't he be happy? He was playing football for his favourite club in the world!

Harry's season started in Belgium at Eurofoot. Ryan, Andros and Steven had all gone out on loan, so he was suddenly a senior member of the youth squad.

'A lot of excellent players have played in this tournament,' coach Alex Inglethorpe told them. 'This is going to be a great experience for all of you. We will be playing a lot of games while we're out here, so get ready to test your fitness!'

After his successful trips to Mexico and Switzerland, Harry couldn't wait for his next international adventure. He was a year older now and a much better striker. The tournament schedule was really tiring but Harry scored three goals in his first four games.

'You're on fire!' his strike partner Kudus Oyenuga cheered as they celebrated their win over Dutch team Willem II.

In the end, Tottenham didn't reach the semi-finals but Harry had his shooting boots on, ready for the Premier Academy League to begin. Or so he thought, anyway. But after four matches, he still hadn't scored.

'Just be patient,' Kudus kept telling him.

It was easy for Kudus to say; he had already found the net three times. 'But scoring goals is what I do best!' Harry argued.

'I think you're just trying too hard,' Tom Carroll, their tiny midfield playmaker, suggested. 'Just relax and I bet the goals will come.'

Harry was grateful for his teammates' support and advice. He scored in his next match against Fulham and once he started, he didn't stop. After two free-kick strikes against Watford, first-team coach Harry Redknapp picked him as a sub for the League Cup match against Everton.

'No way! This is too good to be true,' Harry said when he saw the squad list. His name was there next to top professionals like Jermaine Jenas and Vedran Ćorluka.

Alex laughed. 'No, it's for real! Just don't get your hopes up; you probably won't get off the bench.'

Harry didn't come on, but he got to train with his heroes and share a dressing room with them. The experience inspired him to keep working hard. He could feel himself getting closer and closer to his Tottenham dream.

By Christmas, Harry was the Under-18s top scorer

with nine goals, and the new academy captain.

'Alex always had a good feeling about you,' John McDermott said as he congratulated Harry. 'You're certainly proving him right these days! If you keep it up, the future is yours.'

Harry celebrated by scoring his first hat-trick of the season against Coventry City. And the great news just kept coming. In January 2010, he was called up to the England Under-17s for the Algarve Tournament in Portugal.

'Welcome!' the coach John Peacock said at his first squad meeting. 'I guess you must know a lot of these guys from the Premier Academy League?'

'Yes,' Harry replied, trying to hide his nerves. He had played against Benik Afobe, Ross Barkley and Nathaniel Chalobah before but they probably didn't even remember him. He was the new kid and he suddenly felt very shy. Luckily, his new teammates were very friendly.

'Nice to meet you, we needed a new striker,' Nathaniel grinned. 'Benik already thinks he's Thierry Henry!'

Harry soon felt like one of the gang. Off the pitch, they had lots of fun together but on the pitch, they were a focused team. The Under-17 European Championships were only a few months away, and so the Algarve Tournament was a chance for players to secure their places.

As he walked onto the pitch wearing the Three Lions on his shirt for the first time, Harry had to pinch himself to check that he wasn't dreaming. A few years earlier, Spurs had been close to letting him go – but now look at him! It was hard to believe. Harry didn't score against France or Ukraine but he would never forget those matches. He was an England youth international now.

Harry knew that if he played well until May, he had a chance of going to the Euros in Liechtenstein. That's what he wanted more than anything. He kept scoring goals for the Tottenham Under-18s and the Reserves, and crossed his fingers. He finished with eighteen goals in only twenty-two Premier Academy League games. Surely that would be enough to make the England squad?

In the end, Harry never found out because he was too ill to go to the tournament. Instead of representing his country at the Euros, he had to sit at home and watch Nathaniel, Ross and Benik winning without him. When England beat Spain in the final, Harry was both delighted and devastated.

'Congratulations, guys!' he texted his teammates but inside, he was very jealous. He should have been there with them, lifting the trophy.

'You'll get more chances,' his mum told him as he lay on the sofa feeling sorry for himself.

It didn't seem that way at the time, but Harry always bounced back from disappointments.
There was a new season to prepare for, and a first professional Tottenham contract to sign. That was more than enough to lift him out of his bad mood.
It was the best feeling in the world as he signed his name on the papers.

'Thanks for always believing in me,' Harry told Alex as they chatted afterwards. 'I couldn't have done this without you.'

His Under-18s coach shook his head. 'You did it all

yourself but you haven't achieved anything yet, kid. The next step is the hardest but you've got what it takes.'

Harry smiled. It was true; he wouldn't give up until he made it into the Spurs first team.

CHAPTER 13

EXPERIENCE NEEDED

At seventeen, Harry was on his way to becoming
a Spurs superstar but he still had a lot to learn.
Luckily, there were plenty of teachers around him at
Tottenham. In the Reserves, he often played alongside
first team stars who were recovering from injuries, like
David Bentley and Robbie Keane. Harry loved those
matches. He was always watching and listening for
new tips.

'If you need to, take a touch but if you hit it early,
you might catch the keeper out.'

'Don't just assume that he's going to catch it. Get
there in case he drops it!'

By 2010, Harry was also training regularly with

Harry Redknapp's squad. It was hard to believe that he was sharing a pitch with world-class players like Gareth Bale, Luka Modrić and Rafael van der Vaart. But best of all, Harry was working with his hero, Jermain Defoe. Eventually, he plucked up the courage to talk about that street game.

'Oh yeah, I remember that!' Jermain laughed. 'That was you? Wow, I feel *really* old now!'

Jermain became Harry's mentor and invited him to his extra shooting sessions.

'You're a natural goalscorer, H, but it takes more than instinct to become a top striker. You need to practise, practise, practise! What are you aiming for when you shoot?'

It seemed like a really stupid question. 'The goal,' he replied.

'Okay, but what part of the goal? Top corner, bottom corner?'

'Err, I don't know, I guess I–'

Jermain interrupted Harry. 'No, no, no! You've got to know exactly what you're aiming at, H. Before you hit this one, I want you to picture the goal in your head and then aim for the top right corner.'

Harry took his time and placed the ball carefully into the top right corner.

'Good, but you won't get that long to think in a real match.'

Jermain called a young defender over: 'As soon as I play the pass to Harry, close him down.'

Under pressure, Harry hit the target again but his shot went straight down the middle of the goal. 'No, the keeper would have saved that,' Jermain said. So Harry tried again and again until he hit that top right corner.

'Nice! Now let's work on making that space to shoot. Let's hope you're quicker than you look!' Jermain teased.

He was very impressed by Harry's attitude. Not only did he love scoring goals but he also loved improving his game. That was a winning combination. Jermain kept telling the Spurs coaches, 'If you give him a chance, I promise you he'll score!'

But for now, Redknapp already had Jermain, Roman Pavlyuchenko and Peter Crouch in his squad. Harry would have to wait for his chance. He was doing well for the Reserves but was that the best place for him to develop? Spurs' youth coaches didn't think so.

'He's a great kid and a talented player but what's his best position?' Les Ferdinand asked Tim Sherwood.

That was a difficult question. Harry was a natural finisher but he was also good on the ball. He could read the game well as a second striker, linking the midfield and attack.

Sherwood's silence proved Ferdinand's point. 'That's the big issue. He's a goalscorer but he's not strong enough to battle against big centre-backs.'

'Not yet, no.'

'Plus, he's not quick enough to get in behind the defence.'

This time, Sherwood disagreed. 'He's quicker than he looks and he's lethal in the box.'

After a long discussion, the Spurs coaches agreed on an action plan – Harry would go out on loan in January 2011 to a lower league club.

'We've spoken to Leyton Orient and they want to take you for the rest of the season,' Sherwood told him in a meeting.

At first, Harry was surprised and upset. He didn't want to leave Tottenham, even if it was only for a few months.

'Look, kid, a spell in League One will be good for you,' Sherwood explained. 'You need first-team experience and you're not going to get that here at the moment, I'm afraid. We also need to toughen you up a bit, put some muscle on that skinny frame. Don't worry – we're not going to forget about you!'

Harry spoke to his parents and he spoke to his teammates. They all agreed that it was a good idea.

'Everyone goes out on loan at some point,' Ryan told him. 'It's better than being stuck in the Reserves, trust me!'

'I was at Orient last season,' Andros told him. 'It's a good club and they'll look after you. At least, Spurs aren't asking you to go miles from home. Leyton is just up the road!'

They were right, of course. If a loan move to Leyton Orient would help him to improve and get into the Tottenham first team, Harry would go. It really helped that he wouldn't be going alone.

'Let's do this!' Tom cheered as they travelled to their first training session together.

CHAPTER 14

LEYTON ORIENT

Rochdale's pitch looked bad even before the match kicked off. Where had all the grass gone? As the Leyton Orient squad warmed up, they kept away from the boggy penalty areas and corners. They didn't want to make things worse. When Harry tried a short sprint, his boots sank into the squelch and it was difficult to lift them out. How was he supposed to make runs into the box?

Orient's striker Scott McGleish watched and laughed. 'Welcome to League One, kid!'

The Spotland Stadium was certainly no White Hart Lane. After seventy minutes of football and heavy rain, it looked more like a mud bath than a pitch. On the bench, Harry sat with his hood up, shaking his legs to keep warm. The score was 1–1, perfect for a super sub...

'Harry, you're coming on!' the assistant manager Kevin Nugent turned and shouted.

This was it – his Leyton Orient debut. Harry jumped to his feet and took off his tracksuit. As he waited on the touchline, he didn't even notice the rain falling. He was so focused on making a good first impression for his new club.

'It's fun out there today!' Scott joked, high-fiving Harry as he left the field.

Harry grinned and ran on. He was desperate to make a difference, either by scoring or creating the winning goal. He chased after every ball but before he knew it, the final whistle went.

'Well done, lad,' his manager Russell Slade said, slapping his wet, muddy back.

Harry had enjoyed his first short battle against the big League One centre-backs. They wanted to teach the Premier League youngster about 'real football', and he wanted to show them that this Premier League youngster could cope with 'real football'. Scott was right; it *was* fun!

'So, how did you find it?' Kevin asked back in the dressing room. Alex Inglethorpe had left him in charge of Harry and Tom during their loan spell at the club.

'It's different, that's for sure!' Harry replied after a nice hot shower. 'I need to get stronger but I'm ready for the challenge.'

Orient's assistant manager was impressed. The kid had a great attitude and that was very important in professional football. He could see the hunger in his eyes.

Harry was picked to start the next home game against Sheffield Wednesday. It was a big responsibility for a seventeen-year-old. He fought hard up front but it wasn't easy against really experienced defenders. At half-time, it was still 0–0.

'You're causing them lots of problems,' Kevin reassured him. 'Keep doing what you're doing and be patient.'

Harry felt more confident as he ran out for the second half. He had fifteen, or maybe twenty, minutes to grab a goal before the manager took him off. 'I can do this,' he told himself.

When Orient took the lead, the whole team breathed a sigh of relief. They started passing the ball around nicely and creating more chances. Harry only needed one. When it arrived, he steadied himself and placed his shot carefully.

Goooooooooooooooaaaaaaaaaaaaaaaaaallllllllllllllllllllllllllll!!!!!!!!!!!!!!!!!!!!

He had scored on his full debut! Harry ran towards the Orient fans to celebrate. It felt like the start of big things.

'You're one of us now!' Scott cheered as they high-fived on the touchline.

*

'So, how is Harry getting on?' Alex asked Kevin when they met up a few months later.

The Orient assistant manager chuckled. 'That boy's a real fighter, isn't he? His legs are no bigger than matchsticks but he's fearless. He's good in front of goal, too.'

'What about that red card against Huddersfield?'

Kevin shook his head. 'The second yellow was very harsh,' he explained. 'I'm not sure he even touched the guy! You know that's not Harry's way. He's one of the good guys.'

Tottenham's youth coach nodded. He knew all about Harry's character. Some youngsters really struggled to adapt to new environments, but clearly not him. Alex never had any doubt that Harry would make the most of his first-team experience.

With Orient chasing a playoff spot, Harry was back on the bench for the last few matches of the season. It wasn't where he wanted to be but he was pretty pleased with his record of five goals in eighteen games. It was a decent start to his professional career.

'Welcome back, stranger!' Ryan joked when Harry returned to Tottenham in May.

Despite going out on loan, he had never really left his beloved club. After training with Orient, Harry often went back to do extra sessions with the Spurs Under-21s. They couldn't get rid of him that easily.

Over the summer of 2011, Redknapp sold Peter Crouch and Robbie Keane, and replaced them with

Emmanuel Adebayor. Harry was feeling positive about his sums.

'Two strikers left and only one came in,' he thought to himself. 'That means one spare spot for me!'

It looked that way at the start of the 2011–12 season. In August, Harry made his Tottenham debut at White Hart Lane, against Hearts in the UEFA Europa League. They were already 5–0 up from the first leg, so Redknapp threw him straight into the starting line-up, with Andros and Tom. Harry had never been so excited.

'I'm keeping Jermain out of the team!' he joked with his brother.

'What shirt number did they give you?' Charlie asked.

'37.'

'And what number is Jermain?'

'18.'

'Well, you're not the star striker yet then, bro!'

But Harry wasn't giving up until he *was* Tottenham's star striker. In the twenty-eighth minute, he chased after Tom's brilliant through-ball. It was a

move that they had practised so many times in the
Spurs youth teams. Harry got there first, just ahead of
the Hearts keeper, who tripped him. Penalty!

Harry picked himself up and walked over to get
the ball. This was *his* penalty, a great opportunity to
score on his Spurs debut. He placed it down on the
spot and took a few steps back. He tried to ignore the
goalkeeper bouncing on his line. He pictured the goal
in his head, just like Jermain had taught him.

After a deep breath, he ran towards the ball but
suddenly, doubts crept into his head. Was it a bad idea
to shoot bottom left like he usually did? He paused
just before he kicked it and that gave the keeper time
to make the save. Harry ran in for the rebound but it
was no use; he had missed the penalty.

Harry was devastated but he didn't stand there with
his head in his hands. The nightmares could wait until
after the match. For now, he kept hunting for his next
chance to become a Tottenham hero…

CHAPTER 15

MILLWALL

'Go out there and score!' Jermain shouted as Harry ran on to replace him.

Tottenham were already 3–0 up against Shamrock Rovers. There was still time for him to grab a fourth.

Danny Rose's cross flew over Harry's head but Andros was there at the back post. As he knocked it down, Harry reacted first and shot past the defender on the line.

Goooooooooooooooooaaaaaaaaaaaaaaaallllllllllllllllll llllll!!!!!!!!!!!!!!!!!!!!!!

Harry turned away to celebrate with Andros. What a feeling! He roared up at the sky. He was a Tottenham goalscorer now, and he could put that awful penalty miss behind him.

Unfortunately, however, that was the end of Tottenham's Europa League campaign. It was a real blow for their young players because the tournament was their big chance to shine. What would happen now? There wasn't space for them in Spurs' Premier League squad, so they would either have to go back to the Reserves or out on loan again.

'Right now, I just want to play week in week out,' Harry told his dad. 'I don't care where!'

Pat smiled. 'Be careful what you wish for. You wouldn't like the cold winters in Russia!'

In the end, Harry and Ryan were sent on loan to Millwall in January 2012. The Lions were fighting to stay in the Championship and they needed goals.

'We only scored one goal in the whole of December,' Harry's new manager Kenny Jackett moaned. 'We played five matches, that's over 450 minutes of football!'

Harry's job was clear and he couldn't wait to help his new team. In his Millwall debut against Bristol City, he had a few chances to score but he couldn't get past former England goalkeeper David James.

When City won the match with a last-minute goal, Harry couldn't believe it. He trudged off the pitch with tears in his eyes.

'Hard luck, kid,' Jackett said, putting an arm around his shoulder. 'You played well. The goals will come.'

His new strike partner, Andy Keogh, gave him similar advice. 'Just forget about the misses. If you keep thinking about them, you'll never score!'

The Millwall players and coaches liked Harry and they wanted him to do well. Despite his talent, he wasn't an arrogant wonderkid who thought he was way too good for them. He was a friendly guy, who worked hard for the team and always wanted to improve.

But six weeks later, Harry was still waiting for his first league goal for Millwall. It was the longest drought of his whole life. What was going wrong? Why couldn't he just put the ball in the net? Eventually, he did it away at Burnley.

He made the perfect run and James Henry played the perfect pass. Harry was through on goal. Surely, he couldn't miss this one! The goalkeeper rushed out to stop him but he stayed calm and used his side foot to guide the ball into the bottom corner.

Goooooooooooooooooaaaaaaaaaaaaaaaaaallllllllllllllllllll llllllllll!!!!!!!!!!!!!!!!!!!

Harry pumped his fists and jumped into the air. It was finally over! James threw himself into Harry's arms.

'Thanks mate!' Millwall's new goalscorer shouted above the noise of the fans. 'There's no stopping me now!'

With his confidence back, Harry became a goal machine once more. The Championship defenders just couldn't handle his movement. He was deadly in the penalty area, hitting the target with every shot and header. But he was also brilliant when he played behind the striker. In a deeper role, he had the technique and vision to set up goals.

'Cheers!' Andy shouted after scoring from his perfect pass.

Harry also loved to hit a long-range rocket. Against Peterborough, he spun away from his marker and chased after the ball. It was bouncing high and he was on his weaker left foot, but Harry was feeling bold. Why not? Jermain and Robbie had taught him a very important lesson at Tottenham – if you shoot early, the keeper won't be ready. Harry struck his shot powerfully and accurately into the far corner.

Gooooooooooooooooooooooaaaaaaaaaaaaaaaaalllllllll llllllllllllllllll!!!!!!!!!!!!!!

Harry ran towards the fans and slid across the grass on his knees.

'You're on fire!' Andy cheered as they celebrated together.

With his nine goals, Harry won Millwall's Young Player of the Season award. It was a proud moment for him and a nice way to say goodbye to the club.

'We're going to miss you!' Jackett told him after his last training session. 'It's been a pleasure working with you. Good luck back at Spurs – you're going to be great.'

Harry was sad to leave Millwall but he was also excited about returning to Tottenham. He had learnt a lot from his loan experience. He was now a stronger player, both physically and mentally. It was much harder to push him off the ball, and much harder to stop him scoring.

'2012–13 is going to be my season!' Harry told his family confidently.

But first, he was off to play for England at the UEFA European Under-19 Championships in Estonia. Nathaniel, Benik and Ross were in the squad too, along with some exciting new players: Eric Dier was a tough defender and Nathan Redmond was a tricky winger.

'There's no reason why we can't win this!' their manager Noel Blake told them.

Although he wore the Number 10 shirt, Harry played in midfield behind Benik and Nathan. He enjoyed his playmaker role but it made it harder for him to do his favourite thing – scoring goals. After a draw against Croatia and a win over Serbia, England needed to beat France to reach the semi-finals.

As the corner came in, most of the England attackers charged towards the goal. But not Harry. He waited around the penalty spot because he had noticed that the French goalkeeper wasn't very good at catching crosses. When he fumbled the ball, it fell straight to Harry, who was totally unmarked. He calmly volleyed it into the net.

Goooooooooooooooooooooaaaaaaaaaaaaaaaalllllllllllllll llllllllllll!!!!!!!!!!!!!!!!!!!!!!

2–1 to England! Harry pumped his fists and pointed up at the sky. He was delighted to score such an important goal for his country.

'You're a genius!' Eric cheered as the whole team celebrated.

Unfortunately, Harry wasn't there to be England's hero in the semi-final against Greece. He had to watch from the bench as his teammates lost in extra-time. It was such a horrible way to crash out of the tournament.

'At least we've got the Under-20 World Cup next summer!' Harry said, trying to make everyone feel a little bit better.

He focused once again on his top target – breaking into the Tottenham first team.

CHAPTER 16

TOUGH TIMES

On the opening day of the 2013–14 season, Harry travelled up to Newcastle with the Tottenham squad. New manager André Villas-Boas wanted to give his young players a chance. Jake Livermore started the match, and Harry and Andros waited impatiently on the subs bench. Would this be the day when they made their Premier League debuts?

'Is it bad to hope that someone gets injured?' Andros joked.

With ten minutes to go, Newcastle scored a penalty to make it 2–1. Harry's heart was racing; surely, this was going to be his moment. Tottenham needed to score again and he was the only striker on the bench.

'Harry, you're coming on!'

He quickly took off his yellow bib, and then his grey tracksuit. He pulled up his socks and re-laced his boots. He tucked his navy-blue Spurs shirt into his white shorts. '37 KANE' was ready for action.

'Good luck!' Andros said as Harry walked down to the touchline.

'Get a goal!' Villas-Boas said as Harry waited to come on.

'Let's do this!' Jermain cheered as Harry ran on to join him up front.

Harry had less than ten minutes to score and become an instant Spurs hero. Anything was possible but Newcastle were in control of the game. Harry's Premier League debut was over before he'd really touched the ball.

'Don't worry, that was just a first taste of the action,' Jermain promised him.

Harry hoped that his mentor was right. He shook hands with his opponents and the match officials. Then he walked over to clap the Tottenham fans in the away stand. He had done his best to save the day for his club.

He couldn't wait for his next chance to play but he wasn't even a substitute for their next match against West Brom. With Emmanuel Adebayor back in the team, he was back in the Reserves. Harry was disappointed but he didn't give up.

'I'm still only nineteen,' he told himself. 'I've got plenty of time to shine.'

A few days later, he joined Norwich City on loan for the rest of the season. The Canaries were in the Premier League, so this was a great opportunity to show Spurs that he was good enough to play at the top level.

'Bring it on!' he told his new manager Chris Hughton.

Against West Ham, Harry came on with twenty minutes to go. That gave him plenty of time to score. He dribbled forward, cut inside and curled the ball just wide of the post.

'So close!' Harry groaned, putting his hands on his head.

Minutes later, he beat the West Ham right-back and

pulled the ball back to Robert Snodgrass... but his shot was blocked on the line! Somehow, the match finished 0–0 but Harry was happy with his debut.

Afterwards, Hughton told the media, 'I think Kane will be a super player'.

Harry was delighted with the praise. His first start for Norwich soon arrived against Doncaster in the League Cup. He couldn't wait.

'I'm definitely going to score!' he told his teammates.

Sadly, Harry didn't score and he only lasted fifty minutes. He tried to carry on but he couldn't; his foot was way too painful. He winced and limped off the pitch.

'What happened?' his brother asked as he rested on the sofa back at home.

'I've fractured a metatarsal,' Harry explained.

'Isn't that what Becks did before the 2002 World Cup?' Charlie joked, trying to cheer his brother up. 'You've got to stop copying him!'

Harry smiled, but he was dreading the surgery and then the months without football. It would drive him crazy.

'You're a strong character,' Alex Inglethorpe told him when he returned to Tottenham, 'and you're going to come back even stronger!'

Harry's new girlfriend helped to take his mind off his injury. He and Katie had gone to the same primary and secondary schools but it was only later that they started dating. They got on really well and made each other laugh, even during the tough times.

Harry spent October and November in the gym, slowly getting his foot ready to play football again. It was long, boring work but he had to do it if he wanted to be playing again before the new year.

That was his big aim. In December, Harry started training with the first team again, and starring for the Reserves.

'I'm feeling good!' Harry told his manager Chris Hughton with a big smile on his face. It was great to be playing football again. He had missed it so much.

On 29 December 2012, he was a sub for the Manchester City match. By half-time, Norwich were losing 2–1.

'They're down to ten men, so let's get forward and

attack,' Hughton told his players in the dressing room. 'We can win this! Harry, you're coming on to replace Steve.'

Harry's eyes lit up. He had been hoping for ten, maybe fifteen, minutes at the end but instead he was going to play the whole second half.

This was his biggest challenge yet. Harry was up against City's captain Vincent Kompany, one of the best centre-backs in the world. These were the big battles that he dreamed about. Harry held the ball up well and made clever runs into space. He didn't score but he was back in business.

'Boss, that was just the start!' he promised Hughton.

Before long, however, Harry was told that he had to return to Tottenham. Villas-Boas wanted a third striker as back-up for Jermain and Emmanuel. Harry was happy to help his club but he wanted to play regular football. What was the point of him being there if he wasn't even getting on the bench? A few weeks later, Villas-Boas sent him back out on loan to Leicester City.

'This is all so confusing!' Harry moaned to Katie. It

had turned into a very topsy-turvy season. 'Do Spurs want me or not?'

It was a question that no-one could answer. Harry tried his best to adapt to another new club but soon after scoring on his home debut against Blackburn, he was dropped from the Leicester starting line-up. It was a massive disappointment. It felt like his career was going backwards.

'If I'm only a sub in the Championship, how am I ever going to make it at Spurs?' he complained to his dad on the phone. Leicester felt like a very long way away from Chingford.

Pat had seen his son looking this sad before. 'Remember when you were fourteen and Tottenham told you that you weren't good enough?' he reminded him. 'You didn't give up back then and you're not going to give up now!'

Harry nodded. He *was* good enough! All he needed was a run of games and a chance to get back into goalscoring form. He just had to believe that the breakthrough would come.

CHAPTER 17

BREAKTHROUGH

'I'm not going anywhere this season,' Harry told Tottenham firmly. After four loan spells, he was determined to stay at the club. 'I'm going to prove that I should be playing here week in, week out!'

Harry wasn't a raw, skinny teenager anymore. He was now twenty years old and he looked like a fit, powerful striker at last. That was thanks to his Football League experience and lots of hard work in the gym to build up his strength. He now had even more power in his shot.

'Looking good, H!' Jermain said in pre-season training. His encouragement was working. Harry was getting better and better.

The 2013 U-20 World Cup in Turkey had been a

very disappointing tournament for England, but not
for Harry. He set up their first goal against Iraq with
a brilliant header, and a few days later scored a great
equaliser against Chile from outside the penalty area.
He hit the ball perfectly into the bottom corner, just
like he did again and again on the training ground.

'What a strike!' England teammate Ross Barkley
said to Harry as they high-fived.

When he returned to England in July, Harry felt
ready to become a Premier League star but again,
Spurs had signed a new striker. Roberto Soldado cost
£26 million after scoring lots of goals for Valencia in
La Liga. Watching his rival in action, Harry didn't
give up. He believed in himself more than ever.

For now, cup matches were Harry's chance to
shine. In the fourth round of the League Cup, Spurs
were heading for a disastrous defeat as opponents
Hull took the lead in extra-time. Could Harry save
the day?

When Jermain passed the ball to him, he had his
back to goal, and needed to turn as quickly as possible.
Harry used his strength and speed to spin cleverly past

his marker. With a second touch, he dribbled towards the penalty area. He was in shooting range now. There were defenders right in front of him, blocking the goal, but he knew exactly where the bottom corner was. Harry could picture it in his head.

Goooooooooooooooooooooaaaaaaaaaaaaaaaaallllllllllll llllllllllllll!!!!!!!!!!!!!!!!!

Yes! Harry pumped his fists and ran towards the fans. The job wasn't done yet but his strike had put Spurs back in the game. When the tie went to penalties, he was one of the first to volunteer.

'I've got this,' he told Spurs manager André Villas-Boas. It was time to make up for that miss in the Europa League.

Harry was Spurs' fifth penalty taker. The pressure was on – he had to score, otherwise they were out of the competition. This time, he felt confident. He had a plan and he was going to stick to it, no matter what. As the goalkeeper dived to the right, Harry slammed his shot straight down the middle. The net bulged – what a relief!

'Well done, you showed a lot of guts there,' Tim

Sherwood told him afterwards, giving him a hug. 'Your time is coming!'

In December 2013, Sherwood took over as Tottenham manager for the rest of the season, after the sacking of Villas-Boas. Harry didn't want to get his hopes up but he knew that his former Under-21 coach believed in his talent. Hopefully, Sherwood would give him more opportunities now. By February, he was coming off the bench more regularly but only because Jermain had signed for Toronto FC in Canada.

'I can't believe you're leaving!' Harry told him as they said goodbye. It was one of his saddest days at White Hart Lane. 'It won't be the same around here without you.'

Jermain smiled. 'It's time for me to move on and it's time for you to step up. I want you to wear this next season.'

It was Jermain's Number 18 shirt. Harry couldn't believe it.

'Wow, are you sure?' he asked. It would be such an honour to follow in his hero's footsteps. 'I promise to do you proud!'

Harry did just that when he finally got his
first Premier League start for Tottenham against
Sunderland in April. After years of waiting, Harry's
time had come. He had never been so nervous in
his life.

'Relax, just do what you do best,' Sherwood told
him before kick-off. He was showing lots of faith in his
young striker. 'Score!'

In the second half, Christian Eriksen curled a
beautiful cross into the six-yard box. As the ball
bounced, Harry made a late run and snuck in ahead
of the centre-back to steer the ball into the bottom
corner.

*Goooooooooooooooooooooaaaaaaaaaaaaaallllllllllllllllllll
llllllllll!!!!!!!!!!!!!!!!!!!!*

Harry was buzzing. With his arms out wide like
an aeroplane, he ran towards the Spurs fans near
the corner flag. He had scored his first Premier League
goal for Tottenham. It was time to celebrate in style.

Aaron Lennon chased after him and jumped up on
his back. 'Yes, mate, what a goal!' he cheered.

Harry was soon in the middle of a big player

hug. He was part of the team now and that was the greatest feeling ever.

There were six more league matches in the season and Harry started all of them. He was full of confidence and full of goals. Against West Bromwich, Aaron dribbled down the right wing and crossed into the six-yard box. Harry jumped highest and headed the ball past the defender on the line.

Goooooooooooooooooooooaaaaaaaaaaaaaaaaalllllllllllllll lllllllllllllll!!!!!!!!!!!!!!!!!!

A week later, they did it again. Aaron crossed the ball and Harry flicked it in. 2–1 to Tottenham!

'You've scored in three games in a row,' Emmanuel Adebayor shouted over the White Hart Lane noise. 'You're a goal machine!'

Harry had also already become a favourite with the fans. They loved nothing more than cheering for their local hero.

He's one of our own,
He's one of our own,
Harry Kane – he's one of our own!

Even an own goal against West Ham didn't stop
Harry's rise. In only six weeks, he had gone from sub
to England's hottest new striker.

'What an end to the season!' Tim Sherwood said as
they walked off the pitch together. 'You'll be playing
for a different manager next season, but don't worry.
If you keep banging in the goals, you're going to be a
Tottenham hero, no matter what!'

CHAPTER 18

EXCITING TIMES AT TOTTENHAM

'Do you think he'll bring in a big new striker?' Harry asked Andros during preseason.

His friend and teammate just shrugged. They would have to wait and see what the new Tottenham manager, Mauricio Pochettino, would do.

As the 2014–15 season kicked off, Spurs had signed a new goalkeeper, some new defenders and a new midfielder. But no new striker! That left only Emmanuel, Roberto and Harry. Harry was feeling really good about his chances. He worked extra hard to impress Pochettino.

'Great work, you've certainly got the desire that I'm looking for in my players,' his manager told him. 'This could be a huge season for you!'

Emmanuel started up front against West Ham in the Premier League but it was Harry, not Roberto, who came on for the last ten minutes. That was a good sign. If he kept scoring goals in other competitions, surely Pochettino would have no choice but to let him play. Harry got five goals in the Europa League and three in the League Cup.

'Kane needs to start in the Premier League!' the fans shouted in the stands.

Harry was making a name for himself with the England Under-21s too. He loved representing his country, especially in the big games. Against France, he positioned himself between the two centre-backs and waited like a predator. When Tom Ince played the through-ball, Harry was already on the move, chasing after it. He was too smart for the French defenders and he chipped his shot over the diving goalkeeper.

Goooooooooooooooooooaaaaaaaaaaaaaaaaaaaalllllllllllll llllllllllll!!!!!!!!!!!!!!

Two minutes later, Tom crossed from the right and Harry was there in the six-yard box to tap the ball into the net.

'That's a proper striker's goal!' his teammate told him as they celebrated together.

Tom was right. Harry was a real goalscorer now, always in the right place at the right time. 'That's thirteen goals in twelve games!' he replied proudly.

By November 2014, there was lots of pressure on Pochettino to give Harry more game-time in the Premier League. Away at Aston Villa, he came on for Emmanuel with half an hour to go.

'Come on, we can still win this match!' his old friend Ryan Mason told him. Soon, Andros was on the pitch too. They were all living their Spurs dreams together.

In injury time, Tottenham won a free kick just outside the penalty area. It was Harry's last chance to save the day for Spurs. Érik Lamela wanted to take it but Harry wasn't letting his big opportunity go. He took a long, deep breath to calm his beating heart. He looked down at the ball and then up at the goal. 'This is going in!' he told himself.

He pumped his legs hard as he ran towards the

ball. He needed as much power as possible. But rather than kicking it with the top of his boot, he kicked it with the side. As the ball swerved through the air, it deflected off the head of a Villa defender and past their scrambling keeper.

Goooooooooooooooooaaaaaaaaaaaaaaaaaalllllllllllllllll lllllllllll!!!!!!!!!!!!!!!!!!!!!

It was the biggest goal that Harry had ever scored. He ran screaming towards the corner flag with all of his teammates behind him. In all the excitement, Harry threw himself down onto the grass for his favourite childhood celebration – the Klinsmann dive. Soon, he was at the bottom of a pile of happy players.

'What a beauty!' Danny Rose cheered in his face.

After scoring the match-winner, Harry was the talk of Tottenham. The fans had a new local hero and they wanted him to play every minute of every game. Against Hull City, Christian Eriksen's free kick hit the post but who was there to score the rebound? Harry!

Even when he didn't score for a few matches, Pochettino stuck with Harry. As a young player, he was still learning about playing at the top level.

'I believe in you,' his manager told him. 'You've got lots of potential and you've got the hunger to improve.'

With Pochettino's support, Harry bounced back against Swansea City. As Christian whipped in the corner kick, Harry made a late run into the box. He leapt high above his marker and powered his header down into the bottom corner.

Goooooooooooooooooooooooaaaaaaaaaaaaallllllllllllllllll llllllll!!!!!!!!!!!!!!!!!!

Once he started scoring, Harry couldn't stop. He was such a natural finisher. On Boxing Day, Harry even scored against one of his old teams. Only eighteen months earlier, he had been sitting on the Leicester City bench. Now, he was causing them all kinds of problems as Tottenham's star striker. With hard work and great support, he was proving everyone wrong yet again.

Pochettino was delighted with his young striker's form but he didn't want him to burn out. 'Get some rest because we've got big games coming up.'

Harry was so excited about the 2015 fixture list ahead – Chelsea on New Year's Day and then a few weeks later, the biggest game of them all: The North London Derby – Tottenham vs Arsenal.

'Don't worry, boss,' he said with a big smile. 'I'll be ready to score some more!'

CHAPTER 19

GOALS, GOALS AND MORE GOALS

As the Tottenham team walked out of the tunnel at White Hart Lane, Harry was second in line, right behind their goalkeeper and captain, Hugo Lloris. He had come so far in the last eighteen months – it was still hard to believe. There were thousands of fans in the stadium, cheering loudly for their team, and cheering loudly for him.

> *He's one of our own,*
> *He's one of our own,*
> *Harry Kane – he's one of our own!*

Harry looked down at the young mascot who was

holding his hand. Ten years before, that had been one of his biggest dreams – to walk out on to the pitch with his Spurs heroes. Now, he was the Spurs hero, so what was his new dream? Goals, goals and more goals, starting against their London rivals Chelsea.

'Come on, we can't let them beat us again!' Harry shouted to Ryan and Andros. They were all fired up and ready to win.

Chelsea took the lead, but Harry didn't let his head drop. It just made him even more determined to score. He got the ball on the left wing and dribbled infield. He beat one player and then shrugged off another. He only had one thing on his mind – goals. When he was just outside the penalty area, he looked up.

He was still a long way out and there were lots of Chelsea players in his way, but Harry could shoot from anywhere. The Premier League would soon know just how lethal he was. For now, however, the defenders gave him just enough space. His low, powerful strike skidded across the wet grass, past the keeper and right into the bottom corner.

*Goooooooooooooooaaaaaaaaaaaaaaaalllllllllllllllllllllll
lllll!!!!!!!!!!!!!!!!!!!!!!!*

Game on! Harry ran towards the Tottenham fans
and jumped into the air. He was used to scoring goals
now, but this was one of his best and most important.

'You could outshoot a cowboy!' Kyle Walker joked
as he climbed up on Harry's back.

At half-time, Spurs were winning 3–1 but Harry
wanted more. 'We're not safe yet,' he warned his
teammates. 'We've got to keep going!'

As the pass came towards him, Harry was just
inside the Chelsea box with his back to goal. It didn't
look dangerous at first but one lovely touch and spin
later, it was very dangerous indeed. Harry stayed calm
and placed his shot past the goalkeeper. It was like
he'd been scoring top goals for years.

'Kane, that's gorgeous!' the TV commentator
shouted. 'How good is *he*?'

The answer was: unstoppable. Even one of the best
defences in the world couldn't handle him. The match
finished 5–3. It was a famous victory for Tottenham

and Harry was their hero. After shaking hands with the Chelsea players, he walked around the pitch, clapping the supporters. Harry loved making them happy.

'If we play like that against Arsenal, we'll win that too!' he told Andros.

Harry got ready for the big North London Derby by scoring goals, goals and more goals. The timing was perfect; he was in the best form of his life just as Arsenal were coming to White Hart Lane. Revenge would be so sweet for Harry. Arsenal would soon realise their big mistake in letting him go.

After five minutes, Harry cut in from the left and curled a brilliant shot towards goal. He got ready to celebrate because the ball was heading for the bottom corner yet again. But the Arsenal keeper made a great save to tip it just round the post. So close! Harry put his hands to his head for a second but then kept going. If at first you don't score, shoot, shoot again.

At half-time, Tottenham were losing 1–0. 'We're still in this game,' Pochettino told his players in the dressing room. 'If we keep creating chances, we'll score!'

When Érik took the corner, Harry stood lurking near the back post. He was waiting for the rebound. The keeper saved Mousa Dembélé's header but the ball bounced down in the box. Before the Arsenal defenders could react, Harry pounced to sweep it into the net.

Goooooooooooooooooooaaaaaaaaaaaaaaalllllllllllllllllll llllllll!!!!!!!!!!!!!!!!!!!

Harry roared and pumped his fists. Scoring for Spurs against Arsenal meant the world to him. He had dreamed about it ever since his first trip to White Hart Lane.

'Right, let's go and win this now!' Harry told his teammates.

With five minutes to go, it looked like it was going to be a draw. As Nabil Benteleb's cross drifted into the box, Harry's eyes never left the ball. He took a couple of steps backwards and then leapt high above Laurent Koscielny. It was a very difficult chance. To score, his header would have to be really powerful and really accurate.

As soon as the ball left his head, Harry knew that he had got the angle right. It was looping towards the corner but would the keeper have time to stop it? No, Harry's perfect technique gave David Ospina no chance.

Goooooooooooooooooaaaaaaaaaaaaaaaaalllllllllllllllllll llll!!!!!!!!!!!!!!!!!!!!

As the ball landed in the net, Harry turned away to celebrate. What a moment! With the adrenaline flooding through his veins, he slid across the grass, screaming. As he looked up, he could see the Spurs fans going crazy in the crowd. All that joy was because of him!

The final minutes felt like hours but eventually, the referee blew the final whistle. Tottenham 2, Arsenal 1! The party went on and on, both down on the pitch and up in the stands.

'I might as well retire now!' Harry joked with Ryan. 'Nothing will ever beat scoring the winner in the North London Derby.'

'Not even playing for England?' his teammate asked him. 'Mate, Roy Hodgson would be a fool not to call you up to the squad!'

Harry was desperate to play for his country. Like his hero Becks, he wanted to be the national captain one day. After doing well for the Under-21s, he was now ready to step up into the senior team. He had won both the January and February Premier League Player of the Month awards. Then, in March, Harry got the call he had been waiting for.

'I'm in!' he told his partner Katie excitedly. He wanted to tell the whole world.

'In what?' she asked. 'What are you talking about?'

'The England squad!'

The amazing news spread throughout his family. Everyone wanted a ticket to watch his international debut.

'I might not even play!' Harry warned them, but they didn't care.

He was glad to see that lots of his Tottenham teammates were in the England team too. Training with superstars like Wayne Rooney and Gary Cahill would be a lot less scary with Kyle, Andros and Danny by his side. A week later, Ryan also joined the Spurs gang.

'Thank goodness Fabian Delph got injured!' he laughed. 'I was gutted to be the only one left behind.'

They were all named as substitutes for the Euro 2016 qualifier against Lithuania at Wembley. But would any of them get to come on and play? They all sat there on the England bench, crossing their fingers and shaking with nerves.

With seventy minutes gone, England were winning 3–0. It was time for Roy Hodgson to give his young players a chance. Harry's England youth teammate Ross Barkley was the first substitute and Harry himself was the second. He was replacing Wayne Rooney.

'Good luck!' Ryan and Andros said, patting him on the back.

Harry tried to forget that he was making his England debut at Wembley. That was something he could enjoy later when the match was over. For now, he just wanted to score.

As Raheem Sterling dribbled down the left wing, Harry took up his favourite striking position near the back post. Raheem's cross came straight towards him;

he couldn't miss. Harry had all the time in the world to place his header past the keeper.

Goooooooooooooooooaaaaaaaaaaaaaaallllllllllllllllllllllllllllllllll!!!!!!!!!!!!!!

In his excitement, Harry bumped straight into the assistant referee. 'Sorry!' he called over his shoulder as he ran towards the corner flag.

'Was that your first touch?' Danny Welbeck asked as they celebrated.

'No, it was my third or fourth,' Harry replied with a cheeky grin. 'But I've only been on the field for about a minute!'

There had been so many highlights for Harry during the 2014–15 season already, but this was the best of all. He had scored for England on his debut. All of his dedication had paid off and he felt so proud of his achievements. Harry's childhood dream had come true.

CHAPTER 20

HARRY AND DELE

'So, do you think you can score as many this season?'
Charlie asked his brother.

Lots of people thought Harry's twenty-one Premier
League goals were a one-off, a fluke. They argued that
the PFA Young Player of the Year wouldn't be as good
in 2015–16 because defenders would know all about
him now. They would mark him out of
the game.

But Harry knew that wasn't true. 'Of course I can.
In fact, I'm aiming for even more this time!'

Charlie smiled. 'Good, because when you scored
those goals against Arsenal, the guys in the pub

bought me drinks all night. Sometimes, it's fun being your brother!'

Harry was still getting used to his fame. It was crazy! Every time he took his Labradors Brady and Wilson out for a walk, there were cameras waiting for him. They even took photos of Katie when she went out shopping.

'Our normal life is over!' she complained as she flicked through the newspapers.

After a very disappointing Euro 2015 with the England Under-21s, Harry was really looking forward to the new season. It would be his first as Tottenham's top striker. With Emmanuel gone, Harry now wore the famous Number 10 shirt. He was following in the footsteps of Spurs legends Jimmy Greaves, Gary Lineker and Harry's own hero, Teddy Sheringham.

Pochettino had strengthened the Spurs squad over the summer. They had signed Son Heung-min, a goal-scoring winger, and Dele Alli, a young attacking midfielder.

Harry and Dele clicked straight away. After a few

training sessions, Dele knew where Harry would run, and Harry knew where to make space for Dele. It was like they had been playing together for years. Soon, they were making up cool goal celebrations.

'It's like you guys are back in the school playground!' captain Hugo Lloris teased, but it was great to see them getting along so well.

Despite all of his excitement, Harry didn't score a single goal in August 2015. The newspapers kept calling him a 'one-season wonder' but that only made him more determined to prove them wrong.

'You're playing well and working hard for the team,' Pochettino reassured him. 'As soon as you get one goal, you'll get your confidence back.'

Against Manchester City, Christian's brilliant free kick bounced back off the post and landed right at Harry's feet. He was in lots of space and the goalkeeper was lying on the ground. Surely he couldn't miss an open goal? Some strikers might have passed the ball carefully into the net to make sure but instead, Harry curled it into the top corner.

Goooooooooooooooaaaaaaaaaaaaaaaalllllllllllllllll lllllll!!!!!!!!!!!!!!!!!!!

Harry was delighted to score but most of all, he was relieved. His goal drought was over. Now, his season could really get started.

'Phew, I thought you were going to blaze that one over the bar!' Dele joked.

After that, Harry and Dele became the Premier League's deadliest double act. Between them, they had power, skill, pace and incredible shooting. By the end of February 2016, Tottenham were only two points behind Leicester City at the top of the table.

'If we keep playing like this, we'll be champions!' Pochettino told his players.

Every single one of them believed it. Spurs had the best defence in the league and were also one of the best attacking sides. Dele, Érik and Christian created lots of chances, and Harry scored lots of goals. It was one big, happy team effort. The pranks and teasing never stopped.

'How long do you have to wear that thing for?'

Dele asked during training one day. 'Halloween was months ago, you know!'

'Very funny,' Harry replied, giving his teammate a friendly punch. He was wearing a plastic face mask to protect his broken nose. 'Who knows, maybe it will bring me luck and I'll wear it forever!'

'Let's hope not!' Christian laughed.

Next up was the game that Harry had been waiting months for – the North London Derby. Could they win it again? Arsenal were only three points behind Spurs, so the match was even more important than usual.

'Come on lads, we've got to win this!' Harry shouted in the dressing room before kick-off, and all of his teammates cheered.

The atmosphere at White Hart Lane was incredible. The fans never stopped singing, even when Tottenham went 1–0 down. They believed that their team would bounce back, especially with Harry up front.

Early in the second half, Harry thought he had scored the equaliser. The goalkeeper saved his vicious shot, but surely he was behind the goal-line?

'That's in!' Harry screamed to the referee. But the technology showed that a tiny part of the ball hadn't crossed the line.

It was very frustrating but there was no point in complaining. Harry would just have to keep shooting until he got the whole ball into the net.

In the end, it was Toby Alderweireld who made it 1–1. Tottenham were playing well, but they needed a second goal to take the lead.

The ball was heading out for an Arsenal goal-kick but Dele managed to reach it and flick it back to his best friend, Harry. It looked like an impossible angle but with the supporters cheering him on, anything seemed possible. In a flash, Harry curled the ball up over the keeper and into the far corner.

Goooooooooooooooooooaaaaaaaaaaaaaaaaaaaaaallllll llllllllllllll!!!!!!!!!!!!!!

It was one of the best goals Harry had ever scored. He felt on top of the world. He took off his mask as he ran and slid across the grass. Dele was right behind him and gave him a big hug.

'Maybe you *should* keep wearing that!' he joked.

Tottenham couldn't quite hold on for another big victory. A draw wasn't the result that Spurs wanted, but Harry would never forget his incredible goal.

'We're still in this title race,' Pochettino urged his disappointed players. 'We just have to win every match until the end of the season.'

Harry and Dele did their best to make their Premier League dream come true. Dele set up both of Harry's goals against Aston Villa and they scored two each against Stoke City. But with three games of the season to go, Tottenham were seven points behind Leicester.

'If we don't beat Chelsea, our season's over,' Harry warned his teammates.

At half-time, it was all going according to plan. Harry scored the first goal and Son made it 2–0. They were cruising to victory but in the second half, they fell apart. All season, the Spurs players had stayed cool and focused but suddenly, they got angry and made silly mistakes. It finished 2–2.

'We threw it away!' Harry groaned as he walked off the pitch. He was absolutely devastated. They had worked so hard all season. And for what?

'We've learnt a lot this year,' Pochettino told his players once everyone had calmed down. 'I know you feel awful right now but you should be so proud of yourselves. Next season, we'll come back stronger and win the league!'

There was one bit of good news that made Harry feel a little better. With twenty-five goals, he had won the Premier League Golden Boot, beating Sergio Agüero and Jamie Vardy.

'And they said I was a one-season wonder!' Harry told his brother Charlie as they played golf together. A smile spread slowly across his face. He loved proving people wrong.

CHAPTER 21

ENGLAND

When Harry first joined the England squad back in 2015, he was really nervous. It was a massive honour to represent his country but there was a lot of pressure too. If he didn't play well, there were lots of other great players that could take his place. Plus, it was scary being the new kid.

'You'll get used to this,' Wayne Rooney reassured him. 'I remember when I first got the call-up. I was only seventeen and it was terrifying! Just try to ignore the talk and enjoy yourself.'

Wayne helped Harry to feel more relaxed around the other senior players. They had fun playing golf and table tennis together. They were nice guys and Harry soon felt like one of the lads.

'France, here we come!' he cheered happily.

England qualified for Euro 2016 with ten wins out of ten. Harry added to his debut goal with a cheeky chip against San Marino and a low strike against Switzerland.

'At this rate, you're going to take my place in the team!' Wayne told him.

Harry shook his head. 'No, we'll play together up front!'

When Roy Hodgson announced his England squad for Euro 2016, Harry's name was there. He was delighted. There were four other strikers – Wayne, Jamie Vardy, Daniel Sturridge and Marcus Rashford – but none of them were scoring as many goals as him.

'You'll definitely play,' his brother Charlie told him.

Harry couldn't wait for his first major international tournament. His body felt pretty tired after a long Premier League season with Tottenham, but nothing was going to stop him.

'I really think we've got a good chance of winning it,' he told Dele, who was in the squad for France too.

His friend was feeling just as confident. 'If we play

like we do for Spurs, we can definitely go all the way!'

Harry and Dele were both in the starting line-up for England's first group match against Russia. With Wayne now playing in midfield, Harry was England's number-one striker. He carried the country's great expectations in his shooting boots.

'I *have* to score!' he told himself as the match kicked off in Marseille.

England dominated the game but after seventy minutes, it was still 0–0. Harry got more and more frustrated. He was struggling to find the burst of pace that got him past Premier League defences. What was going wrong? His legs felt heavy and clumsy.

'Just be patient,' Wayne told him. 'If you keep getting into the right areas, the goal will come.'

When they won a free kick on the edge of the Russia box, Harry stood over the ball with Wayne and his Tottenham teammate Eric Dier. Everyone expected Harry to take it but as he ran up, he dummied the ball. Eric stepped up instead and curled the ball into the top corner. 1–0!

'Thanks for letting me take it,' he said to Harry as

they celebrated the goal.

'No problem!' he replied. England had the lead and that was all that mattered.

But just as they were heading for a winning start to the tournament, Russia scored a late header. As he watched the ball flying towards the top corner, Harry's heart sank. He was very disappointed with the result and with his own performance in particular. It wasn't good enough. If he didn't improve, he would lose his place to Jamie or Daniel or Marcus.

'I believe in you, we all believe in you,' Hodgson told him after the game. 'So, believe in *yourself*!'

Harry tried not to read the player ratings in the English newspapers. Instead, he focused on bouncing back. If he could score a goal against Wales in the next game that would make everything better again.

But at half-time, it was looking like another bad day for Harry and England. He worked hard for the team but his goal-scoring touch was gone. The ball just wouldn't go in. When Gareth Bale scored a free kick to put Wales 1–0 up, Harry feared the worst.

'We need a quick goal in the second half,' Hodgson

told the team in the dressing room. 'Jamie and Daniel, you'll be coming on to replace Harry and Raheem.'

Harry stared down at the floor. Was that the end of his tournament? He was really upset but he had to accept the manager's decision.

Harry watched the second half from the bench and cheered on his teammates. He was a good team player. When Jamie scored the equaliser, he joined in the celebrations. When Daniel scored the winner in injury time, he sprinted to the corner flag to jump on him.

'Get in!' he screamed.

It was only after the final whistle that Harry started worrying again. Had he lost his place in the team, or would he get another chance against Slovakia?

'I'm sorry but I've got to start Daniel and Jamie in the next match,' Hodgson told him. 'Rest up and get ready for the next round. We need you back, firing!'

Without Harry, England couldn't find a goal, but 0–0 was enough to take them through to the Round of 16. He would get one more opportunity to score against Iceland, and he was pumped up for the biggest game of his international career.

It started brilliantly. Raheem was fouled in the box and Wayne scored the penalty. 1–0! It was a huge relief to get an early goal but two minutes later, it was 1–1.

'Come on, focus!' Joe Hart shouted at his teammates.

Harry and Dele both hit powerful long-range strikes that fizzed just over the crossbar. England looked in control of the game, but then Iceland scored again.

'No!' Harry shouted. His dream tournament was turning into an absolute nightmare.

England needed a hero, and quickly. Daniel crossed the ball to Harry in his favourite position near the back post. It was too low for a header so he went for the volley. Harry watched the ball carefully onto his foot and struck it beautifully. Unfortunately, it just wasn't his day, or his tournament. The goalkeeper jumped up high to make a good save. So close! Harry put his hands to his face – he was so desperate to score.

As the minutes ticked by, England started panicking. Harry's free kick flew miles wide. What a disaster! The boos from the fans grew louder.

'Stay calm, we've got plenty of time!' Hodgson
called out from the touchline.

That time, however, ran out. At the final whistle,
the Iceland players celebrated and the England players
sank to their knees. They were out of the Euros after a
terrible, embarrassing defeat.

As he trudged off the pitch, Harry was in shock. It
was the worst feeling ever. He felt like he had really
let his country down. Would they ever forgive him?

To take his mind off the disappointment, Harry
watched American Football and focused on his future
goals. With Tottenham, he would be playing in the
Champions League for the first time, and trying to win
the Premier League title. With England, he would be
playing in the qualifiers for World Cup 2018. There
were lots of exciting challenges ahead.

'I need to make things right!' Harry told himself.

CHAPTER 22

TOTTENHAM FOR THE TITLE?

'Argggghhhhhhhhhhhhhhhhhhh!' Harry screamed as he lay down on the turf. He tried to stay calm but it felt like really bad news. As he waved for the physio, the pain got worse and worse. White Hart Lane went quiet. The Spurs fans waited nervously to see whether their star striker could carry on.

'You're not singing anymore!' the opposing Sunderland fans cheered bitterly.

If only Harry hadn't slid in for the tackle. Tottenham were already winning 1–0 thanks to his goal. That was his job: scoring goals, not making tackles. But Harry always worked hard for the team. As he went to block the Sunderland centre-back, his right ankle twisted awkwardly in the grass. If the injury wasn't too serious, Harry promised himself that he would never defend again.

Unfortunately, it *was* serious. Harry tried to get up and play on but that wasn't possible. He hobbled over to the touchline and sat down again. The Spurs fans cheered and clapped their hero but Harry's match was over. He was carried down the tunnel on a stretcher.

'There's good news and there's bad news,' the doctor told him after the X-rays. 'The good news is that there's no fracture. The bad news is that there's ligament damage.'

Harry wasn't a medical expert but he knew that 'ligament damage' meant no football for a while. 'How long will I be out of action?' he asked, fearing a big number.

'It's too early to say but you should prepare yourself for eight weeks out. Hopefully, it won't be that long.'

Eight weeks! If everything went well, Harry would be back before December but it was still a big blow. His 2016–17 season had only just started. He had only played in one Champions League match. Tottenham needed him.

'Who's going to get all our goals now?' he asked.

'Without you hogging all the chances, I'll score loads more!' Dele replied.

It was good to have Katie and his teammates around to cheer Harry up. It was going to be a boring, difficult couple of months for him. He would just have to recover as quickly as possible. To keep himself going, Harry picked out a key date in the calendar: 6 November. The North London Derby – that was what he was aiming for.

'I always score against Arsenal!' Harry reminded everyone.

Thanks to lots of hard work in the gym, he made it just in time. Harry was delighted to be back on the pitch, even if he wasn't at his best. Early in the second half, Tottenham won a penalty and Harry quickly grabbed the ball. It was the perfect chance to get a comeback goal.

He took a long, deep breath and waited for the referee's whistle. As the Arsenal keeper dived to his left, Harry placed it down the middle.

*Goooooooooooooooooaaaaaaaaaaaaaaalllllllllllllllll
lllll!!!!!!!!!!!!!!!!!!!!!*

He was back! Harry pumped his fists at the crowd
as his teammates jumped on him.

'What a cool finish!' Son cheered.

Harry didn't last the full match, but he was pleased
with his return. 'If I want to win the Golden Boot
again, I've got some catching up to do!' he told
Pochettino.

Tottenham got knocked out in the Champions
League Group Stage, but Harry still had time to grab
his first goals in the competition.

'Never mind, we've just got to focus on the Premier
League title now,' he told Dele. 'We'll conquer Europe
next year!'

After all his goals, Harry became a transfer target
for Real Madrid and Manchester United. Tottenham
wanted to keep their local hero for as long as possible,
so they offered Harry a big new contract until 2020.
Saying no didn't even cross his mind.

'I can't leave!' Harry said happily. 'This is my home
and we've got trophies to win.'

To celebrate, he went on another scoring spree. Two against Watford, three against West Brom, three against Stoke, two against Everton. By March, he was up to nineteen goals and at the top of the goal-scoring charts again.

'Congratulations, you're back where you belong,' Katie told him.

Harry was pleased but the Premier League title was his number one aim. Spurs were in second place behind Chelsea. Harry would give his all to catch them.

For Harry, winning the 2017 FA Cup was aim number two. In the quarter-finals, Tottenham faced his old club Millwall. So much had changed in the five years since his loan spell there. He would always be grateful to the Lions for their support but that didn't mean he would take it easy on them. Trophies always came first.

As soon as the ball came to him, Harry shot at goal. The Millwall keeper saved it but Harry didn't even notice. He was lying on the grass in agony.

'Is it your right ankle again?' the physio asked after rushing over to him.

Harry just nodded. Was it the same injury all over again? He couldn't bear to think about another eight weeks on the sidelines. He managed to limp off the pitch and down the tunnel. He didn't need to use the stretcher this time and that was a good sign.

'There is ligament damage,' the doctors confirmed, 'but it's not as serious as before. We'll do our best to get you back for the semi-final.'

With a target to aim for, Harry was determined to recover in time. He was back in action two weeks before their big cup match against Chelsea. There was even time for him to score a goal.

'See, I'm feeling sharp!' he promised Pochettino. There was no way that he could miss playing in the FA Cup semi-final. He was a big game player and his team needed him.

The atmosphere at Wembley was electric. As usual, Harry was the second Spurs player out of the tunnel. As he looked up, he could see big blocks of white in the crowd.

'*Tottenham! Tottenham! Tottenham!*'

If the stadium was this loud for the semi-final, what

would the final be like? But Harry couldn't get ahead of himself. He had to focus on beating Chelsea first.

The Blues took the lead but with Harry on the pitch, Spurs were always in the game. He stayed onside at the front post to flick on Christian's low cross. Thanks to his clever touch, the ball flew right into the bottom corner.

Goooooooooooooooooooaaaaaaaaaaaaaaaaaalllllllllllll lllllllllllllllll!!!!!!!!!!!!

'It's like you've got eyes in the back of your head!' Christian cheered as they hugged.

'Why would I need that?' Harry asked. 'The goal doesn't move – it's always in the same place!'

Despite his best efforts, Chelsea scored two late goals to win 4–2. It was very disappointing but Tottenham's season wasn't over yet.

'We've got five Premier League matches left,' Harry told Dele. 'If we can get all fifteen points, the pressure is on Chelsea.'

The first three points came at White Hart Lane in the North London Derby against Arsenal. Dele got the first goal and Harry scored the second from the

penalty spot. The dream was still alive! But at West
Ham a week later, Spurs fell apart again. Harry, Dele
and Christian tried and tried but they couldn't get
the goal they needed. In the second half, Tottenham
panicked and conceded a silly goal. The 1-0 defeat left
them seven points behind Chelsea.

'No, the title race isn't over yet,' Pochettino told his
players. 'Come on, let's finish on a high!'

There was no chance of Harry relaxing. Even if
he didn't win the Premier League, he could still win
the Golden Boot. He was only three goals behind
Everton's Romelu Lukaku with three games to go.
Harry closed the gap to two with a neat flick against
Manchester United.

'Three goals against Leicester and Hull? I can do
that!' he told Dele.

'But what if Lukaku scores again?'

Dele was right; Harry needed to aim even higher.
Against Leicester, his first goal was a tap-in, his second
was a header and the third was a rocket from the edge
of the penalty area. Harry had another amazing hat-
trick but he wasn't finished yet. In injury time, he got

the ball in the same position and scored again!

Harry was pleased with his four goals but he couldn't help asking himself, 'Why couldn't I do that against West Ham?' He was never satisfied.

Harry would have to think about that later, though. With one game to go, he was on 26 goals and Lukaku was on 24. At the final whistle in the Arsenal vs Everton game, Lukaku was up to 25 goals for Everton thanks to a penalty, but meanwhile Harry was way ahead on 29! With two fantastic finishes and a tap-in, he had grabbed yet another hat-trick against Hull.

'Wow, you were only two goals off the Premier League record,' his proud dad told him. 'And you missed eight games through injury!'

Harry was delighted with his second Golden Boot in a row but it didn't make up for another season without a trophy. Tottenham kept getting so close to glory but would they ever be crowned champions? Harry, the local hero, never stopped believing.

CHAPTER 23

ONE OF EUROPE'S FINEST

Harry jumped up in the England wall but the free kick flew past him and into the top corner. As he watched, his heart sank. Scotland were winning 2–1 at Hampden Park with a few minutes to go.

'Come on, we can't lose this!' Harry shouted to his teammates.

England were unbeaten in qualification for the 2018 World Cup and this, in June 2017, was a key match against their British rivals. It was also Harry's first match as the national captain. For all of these reasons, he refused to let it end in an embarrassing defeat.

With seconds to go, Kyle Walker passed to Raheem Sterling on the left wing. Harry was surrounded by Scottish defenders but he was clever enough to escape. The centre-backs watched Raheem's high cross sail over their heads and thought they were safe. But they weren't. They had missed Harry's brilliant run to the back post.

There wasn't enough time or space to take a touch, so Harry went for a side-foot volley. With incredible technique and composure, he guided his shot past the keeper.

Gooooooooooooooooooooaaaaaaaaaaaallllllllllllllllllll llll!!!!!!!!!!!!!!!

It was another big goal in a big game. Under pressure, Harry hardly ever failed.

'You're a born leader,' England manager Gareth Southgate told him after the match. 'That's why I gave you the captain's armband.'

At twenty-four, Harry wasn't a bright young talent anymore. After three excellent seasons, he was now an experienced player with lots of responsibility for club and country. Now he felt ready to take the next step and become one of Europe's finest.

'I might not have as much skill as Cristiano Ronaldo and Lionel Messi but I can score as many goals,' he told Dele.

Harry was full of ambition ahead of the 2017–18 season. It was time to shine in the Champions League as well as the Premier League. But first, he had to get August out of the way.

'Maybe I should just take the month off!' Harry joked at home with Katie.

No matter how hard he tried and how many shots he took, he just couldn't score. He was trying to ignore all the talk about his August goal curse. Their beautiful baby daughter was certainly helping to take his mind off things.

'Yes, you could stay home and change Ivy's nappies with me!' Katie replied with a smile. She knew that Harry could never stay away from football. He loved it so much.

On 1 September, he travelled with England to play against Malta. 'Don't worry, I've got this,' he told his teammates. 'August is over!'

As Dele twisted and turned in the penalty area, Harry got into space and called for the pass. The goalkeeper rushed out but he calmly slotted the ball into the net.

Goooooooooooooooooooaaaaaaaaaaaaaaaallllllllllllllllll llllllll!!!!!!!!!!!!!!!!!!

On the touchline, Southgate pumped his fists. Tottenham fans all over the world did the same. Their goal machine was back.

'Finally!' Dele teased him. 'What would you do without me?'

Harry was too relieved to fight back. 'Thanks, you're the best!' he replied.

Once he scored one, Harry usually scored two. He did it against Malta and then he did it against Everton in the Premier League. As always, Harry's timing was perfect. Tottenham were about to start their Champions League campaign against German giants Borussia Dortmund.

'They picked the wrong time to face me!' he said confidently.

Harry won the ball on the halfway line, headed it forward and chased after it. He wasn't letting anyone get in his way. As he entered the Dortmund penalty area, the defender tried to push him wide. Harry didn't mind; he could score from any angle! Before the keeper could react, the ball flew past him.

The Tottenham fans went wild.

> *He's one of our own,*
> *He's one of our own,*
> *Harry Kane – he's one of our own!*

Harry went hunting for another goal and he got it.

'He just gets better and better!' the commentator marvelled.

It was Harry's first Champions League double, but he wanted a third. He was always hungry for more goals. With a few minutes to go, Pochettino took him off.

'The hat-trick will have to wait until next week!' he told his star striker, patting him on the back.

The APOEL Nicosia defence was prepared for Harry's arrival but there was nothing that they could do to stop him. He made it look so easy. He scored his first goal with his left foot and the second with his right. There was half an hour left to get his third but he only needed five minutes.

Kieran Trippier curled the ball in from the right and Harry ran from the edge of the box to glance it down into the bottom corner. All that heading practice had been worth it.

Gooooooooooooooooooooooaaaaaaaaaaaaaaalllllllllll llllllllllllll!!!!!!!!!!!!!!

Harry ran towards Kieran and gave him a big hug. He was always grateful for the assists but this one was particularly special. Harry had his first ever Champions League hat-trick.

'That was perfect!' he told Son afterwards, clutching the match ball tightly.

'Yeah, it was a good win,' his teammate replied.

'No, I mean it was a perfect hat-trick,' Harry explained. 'One with my right foot, one with my left, and one with my head. That's the first time I've ever done that!'

Son laughed. 'You score so many goals. How can you remember them all?'

Every single goal was important to Harry and he often watched videos of his matches to help him improve. He never stopped working on his game.

'Is Kane the best striker in Europe right now?' the newspapers asked. Harry had already scored thirty-six goals by September and he still had three months of the year to go!

To keep his feet on the ground, Harry thought back to his early football days. Arsenal had rejected him and Tottenham had nearly done the same. As an eleven-year-old boy, he had told his hero David Beckham that he wanted to play at Wembley for England. Thanks to lots of practice and determination, Harry had achieved that dream and so much more.

His shirt now hung next to Becks' shirt in the hallway at Chingford Foundation School. Harry had the future at his goalscoring feet. He would do everything possible to lead England to World Cup glory in Russia. But before that, Harry was still determined to win trophies with his boyhood club, Tottenham.

CHAPTER 24

FOOTBALL'S COMING HOME

Harry couldn't wait for the biggest challenge of his football career so far. Not only was he on his way to Russia to play in his first World Cup, but the England manager, Gareth Southgate, had also picked him to captain his country.

With Three Lions on his shirt and the armband on his sleeve, could Harry lead his nation to glory again, after fifty-two years of hurt? It looked unlikely. At the 2014 World Cup, England had finished bottom of their group and at Euro 2016, they had lost to Iceland in the second round. Harry, however, was full of confidence – as always.

'I believe we can win the World Cup,' he told the media. 'We're going to fight and give everything we've got.'

The England team spirit was growing stronger and stronger every day. Yes, they were young but they weren't going to let that stop them. They had the talent to succeed and they got on really well together, no matter which Premier League club they played for. Kyle was one of Harry's best friends – so what if he had moved from Tottenham to Manchester City? 'We're all playing for England now!' everyone agreed.

It was time to give the fans something to cheer about. That task began against Tunisia, one of the top African nations. After the peace and quiet of their base camp, the England players finally experienced the amazing World Cup atmosphere. All that noise, all that colour – what a buzz!

'This is it,' Harry told his teammates, 'this is what we've been dreaming about since we were kids!'

With the adrenaline pumping through their bodies, England started brilliantly. John Stones lept up high to head Ashley Young's corner towards the top corner. Surely, it was going in...no, saved! But yet again, Harry was in the right place at the right time for the rebound.

Gooooooooooooooooooooooooooaaaaaaaaaaaaaaaaaaa aaaaaaalllllllllllllllllllllllllllllllllllllll!!!!!!!!!!!!!!!!!!!!!!!

Harry had his first World Cup goal already! He ran towards the corner flag and slid gleefully across the grass. Soon, he was at the bottom of an England team bundle.

When he finally escaped, Harry stood in front of the cheering crowd and held up the Three Lions on his red shirt. 'Come on!' he roared.

Even when Tunisia made it 1–1 from the penalty spot, Harry kept believing.

'There's still plenty of time to score again!'

Even when defenders wrestled him to the ground in the box but the referee shook his head, Harry kept believing.

'We'll find a way!'

Even with seconds to go, Harry kept believing.

'We can do this!'

Harry Maguire flicked Kieran Trippier's corner towards goal. Harry Kane was waiting at the back post, totally unmarked. What a chance to become

England's World Cup hero! He calmly steered his header past the goalkeeper.

Gooooooooooooooooooooooooaaaaaaaaaaaaaaaaaa aaaaaaalllllllllllllllllllllllllllllllllllllll!!!!!!!!!!!!!!!!!!!!

Another game, another two goals for Harry, England's big game player. And in a World Cup, too! It was the best feeling ever.

'H, what would we do without you?' Ashley screamed.

On the bench, Southgate punched the air. What an important goal, what an important win!

England's next victory, against Panama, was a lot more comfortable.

Kieran crossed and John headed home. 1–0!

Harry smashed in an unstoppable penalty. 2–0!

Jesse curled a long-range shot into the top corner. 3–0!

John finished off a brilliant team move. 4–0!

Harry was wrestled to the ground in the box again and this time, the referee pointed to the spot. 5–0!

The England fans couldn't believe what they were seeing, but Harry could.

'This is awesome!' he laughed in the dressing room at half-time. 'More of the same!'

Harry was on a hat-trick, after all. A fifth goal would take him above Belgium's Romelu Lukaku as the top scorer at the 2018 World Cup.

With 30 minutes to go, Harry looked over at the bench and saw Jamie Vardy warming up. He was about to come off – was there time for one last shot? No, but Ruben Loftus-Cheek's shot flicked up flukily off Harry's heel.

Gooooooooooooooooooooooooaaaaaaaaaaaaaaaaaaa aaaaaaalllllllllllllllllllllllllllllllllllll!!!!!!!!!!!!!!!!!!!!!

'H, that's the worst hat-trick ever!' Jesse Lingard joked.

Harry shrugged and smiled. 'Whatever, there's no such thing as a bad hat-trick!'

Every goal counted, especially for a Number 9. Harry would treasure his World Cup matchball forever. With England through to the Round of 16, suddenly the fans were full of hope and excitement:

It's coming home, it's coming home,
It's coming, FOOTBALL'S COMING HOME!

The players, however, had to keep their feet on the ground. A 1–0 defeat to Belgium in the final game of the group stage set up a second-round match against Colombia.

'This is a massive test for us,' Southgate told his players, 'but we're ready!'

Harry battled bravely against the big centre-backs. When he made a run to head Kieran's corner, Carlos Sánchez pushed him to the floor.

'Foul!' Harry cried out.

Penalty! The Colombian players argued for ages with the referee and they even tried to scuff up the spot, but nothing could stop an ice-cold striker like Harry. He just waited calmly and, when the referee blew the whistle, slotted it coolly home.

Goooooooooooooooooooooooooaaaaaaaaaaaaaaaaaa aaaaaaalllllllllllllllllllllllllllllllllllllll!!!!!!!!!!!!!!!!!!!!

What a tournament he was having – that was goal number six already!

England were on their way to the World Cup quarter-finals, but in the last minute, Colombia equalised. As Harry watched the ball cross the goal-line, he put his hands on his head. Oh no, what now?

'Dig deep!' he shouted to his struggling teammates.

Could England win a World Cup penalty shoot-out for the first time ever? They had been practising for weeks. Harry could barely walk but he knew that his nation needed him. As captain, he had to lead by example.

'I'll go first,' he said firmly.

With all eyes on him and a yellow wall of Colombia fans in front of him, Harry stepped up slowly and... SCORED, of course!

He pumped his fist and re-joined his teammates on the half-way line. Even when Jordan Henderson's penalty was saved, Harry knew that it wasn't over. He trusted their other Jordan – Jordan Pickford – to make at least one super save in the shoot-out.

Carlos Bacca ran up and...there was the super save!

Now, Eric Dier just needed to keep cool and...

Goooooooooooooooooooooooooaaaaaaaaaaaaaaaaaaa aaaaaaalllllllllllllllllllllllllllllllllllllll!!!!!!!!!!!!!!!!!!!!

What a moment – England were through to the World Cup quarter-finals after WINNING ON

PENALTIES! Harry raced over to hug his keeper.

'Jordan, you hero!' he screamed. It was time for an even bigger England team bundle.

Was football really coming home? The impossible now seemed possible. Harry watched all the amazing videos of the celebrations back home.

'Look what we've started, lads,' he told his teammates before their quarter-final against Sweden. 'Come on, we can't stop now!'

England weren't ready to go home yet. Harry Maguire scored a thumping header.

'If one Harry doesn't get you, the other one will!' the TV commentator screamed – and then Dele grabbed a second to send England into the World Cup semi-finals for the first time in twenty-eight years. The whole nation was going football crazy!

'Is it coming home?' a journalist asked afterwards.

Harry grinned. 'We'll have to wait and see, but hopefully!'

Against Croatia, England made another brilliant start when Kieran curled a fantastic free-kick into the top corner – 1–0!

It's coming home, it's coming home,
It's coming, FOOTBALL'S COMING HOME!'

Could England score a second goal to settle the
semi-final? Jesse threaded a great pass through to
Harry in the penalty area.

He just had the goalkeeper to beat...SAVED!

He got to the rebound first...OFF THE POST!

Harry couldn't believe his bad luck, and neither
could the fans. England's superstar striker was usually
so lethal!

Croatia fought their way back into the match – 1–1!
Suddenly, the England players looked nervous and
tired. Harry did his best to urge his team on but could
they hang on for penalties? No- in the 110th minute,
Mario Mandžuki´c won it for Croatia.

At the final whistle, Harry sank to his knees,
surrounded by his band of football brothers. They
had all given absolutely everything.

It was devastating to get so close to the final but
they were still a huge success story. They hadn't
brought the World Cup home but they had brought

football home: England had fallen in love with its national team again. Thousands of fans stayed behind in the stadium to clap and cheer for their heroes.

'It hurts a lot,' Harry tweeted later that night. 'We can be proud and we'll be back. Thanks for all your support. #ThreeLions.'

England lost their third place play-off against Belgium but Harry did finish his first World Cup with an individual award – the Golden Boot for top scorer! It was a great achievement, even if it wasn't the team trophy that he really wanted.

There was plenty of time for that. This was just the beginning for Southgate's England side. Harry couldn't wait to lead his country to glory at Euro 2021 and World Cup 2022.

Turn the page for a sneak preview of
another brilliant football story by
Matt and Tom Oldfield. . .

SUPERSTARS: DE BRUYNE AND DELE ALLI

Available now!

CHAPTER 1

MANCHESTER CITY'S MAIN MAN

Stamford Bridge, 30 September 2017

There was great excitement all across the footballing world, but especially around the Stamford Bridge stadium in West London. It was a sell-out for the biggest game of the Premier League season so far – the champions, Chelsea, versus the most entertaining team in England, Manchester City.

So, who would win the battle of the best? Which manager would come out on top: Chelsea's Antonio Conte or City's Pep Guardiola? And which brilliant Belgian would shine the brightest: Chelsea's Eden Hazard or City's midfield maestro, Kevin De Bruyne?

For Kevin, the match meant more than just another three points for his team. Back in 2012, at the age of twenty, he had made the bold move from his Belgian club Genk to Chelsea, with high hopes of becoming 'the next Frank Lampard', or even 'the new Zinedine Zidane'.

Kevin's manager at Chelsea, José Mourinho, had promised him game-time but, instead, he spent two seasons either out on loan, or sitting on the bench. Kevin had always been a stubborn star. He was impatient and strong-willed too. When he saw that he had no chance at Chelsea, he decided to make a name for himself somewhere else. He went to Germany and quickly became 'The King of the Assists' at VfL Wolfsburg.

Now, Kevin was back in England, starring for a new club. He was the best player in the Premier League and Manchester City were the best team too. Kevin had no hard feelings towards his old club but nevertheless, he had a point to prove to some people. It was time to show, once and for all, that he wasn't a 'Chelsea flop'. Five years on, Kevin was a completely different playmaker – older, wiser, and a whole lot better.

'Let's win this, lads!' his captain David Silva clapped and cheered before kick-off.

That wouldn't be easy away at Stamford Bridge, but City were top of the table and playing with so much style and confidence. With Kevin starting every attack in central midfield, Pep's grand plan was working brilliantly. City had thrashed Liverpool 5–0, then Watford 6–0, then Crystal Palace 5–0. Could they thrash Chelsea too?

Kevin dropped deep to get the ball as often as possible. He had two fantastic feet, capable of creating magic. Sometimes, he curled beautiful long passes over the top for City's speedy winger Raheem Sterling to chase. Sometimes, he played clever one-twos with Raheem, David and right-back Kyle Walker. Sometimes he was on the right, sometimes he was on the left, and sometimes he was in the middle. Kevin was everywhere, doing everything to help his team to win.

His first chance to score came from a free kick. He had scored plenty in his career, even one against

Barcelona in the Champions League. This time, however, his Belgian international teammate Thibaut Courtois made a comfortable save.

'Aaaaaaaaaahhhhhhhhh,' the City fans let out a groan of disappointment, like the air escaping from a balloon. Kevin was so talented that they expected him to get it right every time.

'Next time,' he thought to himself as he ran back into position. As the game went on, Kevin, and City, got better and better.

CHANCE! Kevin crossed to Gabriel Jesus but it was intercepted by a Chelsea defender.

CHANCE! Kevin delivered a dangerous corner kick but Gabriel headed wide.

CHANCE! Kevin chipped the ball towards Gabriel but he headed wide again.

The City fans were growing restless in their seats. Their team was creating lots and lots of chances – but without their star striker, Sergio Agüero, who was going to step up and score the winning goal?

Playing in his new deeper midfield role, Kevin hadn't scored yet that season. Pep wanted him to be the team's pass-master, using his amazing X-ray vision to set up goals for other players. But what if they couldn't score?

Kevin could strike a brilliant shot, full of power and swerve. Like his hero Zidane, he was the complete midfielder, and he was determined to prove himself as a big game player. A win against Chelsea would keep City top of the Premier League, above their local rivals, Manchester United. His team needed him more than ever…

'Attack!' Pep shouted from the sidelines. 'Attack!'

So, the next time that Kevin played a quick pass to Gabriel, he kept running forward for the one-two. Kevin got the ball back and burst through the Chelsea midfield. He was just outside the penalty area now, with plenty of space to…

'Shoot!' the City fans urged. 'Shoot!'

It was on his left foot but Kevin didn't really have a weaker foot, just two magic wands. He steadied himself, pulled his leg back and struck the ball sweetly. *Abracadabra!* It flew through the air and over Courtois's outstretched arms.

*Goooooooooooooooooooaaaaaaaaaaaaaaaalllllllllllll
lllllllllll!!!!!!!!!!!!!!!!!!!!!*

'DE BRUYNE!!' the TV commentator cried out.
'Oh, that's special!'

What an important goal! As the ball hit the back
of the net, the City supporters went wild. Kevin ran
towards them, shaking his finger and roaring like a
lion. He was so pumped up with pride and joy. He
wanted to win the Premier League title so much.

On the touchline, Pep punched the air with delight.
Their Brazilian substitute Danilo couldn't contain his
excitement. He ran straight onto the pitch to bump
chests with their hero. Soon, Kevin was at the centre
of a big team hug.

'Come on!' he called out to the supporters and, in
reply, they sang their favourite song:

Ohhhhhhhh! Kevin De Bruyne!
Ohhhhhhhh! Kevin De Bruyne!

It was an amazing moment for Manchester City's
main man, one that he would never forget. Kevin had
scored his team's winning goal, and against Chelsea!
It didn't get any better than that. Back at Stamford

Bridge, the Belgian had showed the world that he was now a superstar.

'Kev, you're the best!' his manager Pep Guardiola said with a huge smile on his face.

Mourinho might not have believed in him at Chelsea, but Guardiola certainly did at Manchester City. And most importantly, Kevin believed in himself. He had always known that he had the talent, the drive and the resilience to reach the very top, even during his early days in Drongen.

Individual

🏆 PFA Young Player of the Year: 2014–15

🏆 Premier League PFA Team of the Year: 2014–15, 2015–16, 2016–17

🏆 Premier League Golden Boot: 2015–16, 2016–17

🏆 World Cup Golden Boot: 2018

KANE

9 **THE FACTS**

NAME: Harry Edward Kane

DATE OF BIRTH: 28 July 1993

AGE: 27

PLACE OF BIRTH: Walthamstow, London

NATIONALITY: England

BEST FRIEND: Dele Alli

CURRENT CLUB: Tottenham

POSITION: ST

THE STATS

Height (cm):	**188**
Club appearances:	**406**
Club goals:	**242**
Club trophies:	**0**
International appearances:	**48**
International goals:	**32**
International trophies:	**0**
Ballon d'Ors:	**0**

★ ★ ★ **HERO RATING: 88** ★ ★ ★

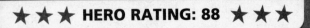

GREATEST MOMENTS

7 APRIL 2014,
TOTTENHAM 5-1 SUNDERLAND

Harry's first Premier League goal was a long time
coming. After four loan spells, he finally got his
chance at Tottenham under Tim Sherwood. Against
Sunderland, Christian Eriksen curled a brilliant ball
into the six-yard box and Harry beat his marker to
score. It was a real striker's finish and a sign of the
great things to come.

2 NOVEMBER 2014,
ASTON VILLA 1-2 TOTTENHAM

This was the goal that changed Harry's career at White Hart Lane. He has definitely scored better goals but this last-minute free kick won the match for Tottenham. Before this, Harry was a substitute. After this, he became the star striker we know and love.

7 FEBRUARY 2015,
TOTTENHAM 2-1 ARSENAL

This was the day that Harry became a true Tottenham hero. In the big North London Derby, he scored two goals to secure a famous victory. Harry's first goal was a tap-in but the second was a world-class header. He used his power and technique to direct the ball right into the corner of the Arsenal goal.

19 MARCH 2015, ENGLAND 4-0 LITHUANIA

It was Harry's international debut at Wembley and he had only been on the pitch for 80 seconds. Raheem Sterling crossed from the left and, as usual, Harry was in the right place at the right time. He scored with a simple header at the back post and then bumped into the match official!

6 OCTOBER 2017, ENGLAND 1-0 SLOVENIA

On a tense night at Wembley, the new England captain led his country to the 2018 World Cup in Russia. In the last minute, Kyle Walker crossed from the right and Harry stretched out his lethal right leg to poke the ball past the keeper.

PLAY LIKE YOUR HEROES

THE HARRY KANE FINISH

STEP 1: Make a clever forward run between the defenders.

STEP 2: When you get the ball, control it perfectly. That first touch is really important!

STEP 3: Use your skill and strength to escape your marker and open up a bit of space to shoot.

STEP 4: Don't wait! Strike the ball as early as possible to surprise the keeper.

STEP 5: Keep it low! When the ball zips across the grass, it's harder for the keeper to save.

STEP 6: Aim for the corner! Picture the goal in your head and pick your spot. Go for the right or the left but never go down the middle.

STEP 7: As the ball hits the back of the net, run towards the fans in the corner with your arms out wide and a big grin on your face.

TEST YOUR KNOWLEDGE

QUESTIONS

1. Who was Harry's first Tottenham hero?

2. What position did Harry first play at Ridgeway Rovers?

3. Which other England legend also played for Ridgeway Rovers?

4. Which three clubs did Harry have trials with when he was a youngster?

5. Name three of Harry's teammates in the Tottenham youth team.

6. How many loan spells did Harry have before settling at Spurs?

7. Who was the Spurs manager when Harry made his first Premier League start?

8. Who gave Harry his Number 18 shirt when he left Tottenham?

9. Harry scored on his England debut – True or False?

10. How many goals did Harry score for England at Euro 2016?

11. How many Premier League Golden Boots has Harry won so far?

Answers below. . . No cheating!

1. Teddy Sheringham 2. Goalkeeper 3. David Beckham 4. Arsenal, Watford and Tottenham 5. Any of Tom Carroll, Jonathan Obika, Kudus Oyenuga, Ryan Mason, Andros Townsend and Steven Caulker 6. Four – Leyton Orient, Millwall, Norwich City and Leicester City 7. Tim Sherwood 8. Jermain Defoe 9. True – Harry scored after only 80 seconds against Lithuania! 10. 0 11. 2